Named One of the Best Books of the Year by:
NPR
The Guardian
The Observer
The Brooklyn Rail
Shelf Awareness
Cultured Vultures

Selected by Emma Watson as an Our Shared Shelf
Book Club Pick
Sunday Times Bestseller
Winner of the British Book Awards:
Nonfiction Narrative Book of the Year
Winner of the Jhalak Prize

More Praise for *Why I'm No Longer
Talking to White People About Race*

"The most important book for me this year." —**Emma
Watson**

"This political, accessible and uncompromising book
has got people talking about race and racism in
Britain." —*The Guardian,* Books of the Year

"A fresh perspective, offering an Anglocentric alternative to the recent status-quo-challenging successes
Get Out and *Dear White People*. This book's probing

analysis and sharp wit certainly make us pray [Eddo-Lodge] will continue talking to white people about race." —*Harper's Bazaar*

"[Eddo-Lodge's] work, which began as a silent scream against white complicity to racism, has shifted the conversation in the U.K . . . Though she may not be talking to white people about race, she has gotten a lot of people to listen." —*Time* magazine

"You don't have to live in the U.K. to recognize the issues of white privilege, class, feminism and structural racism that [Eddo-Lodge] explores in this essential book." —**NPR**

"Reni Eddo-Lodge is that rarest of delights—a young, working-class Black woman from the humble London neighborhood of Tottenham with a voice in public life . . . [This] book is a real eye-opener when it comes to Britain's hidden history of discrimination . . . A book like this matters now." —*Refinery29*

"Eddo-Lodge explores the nuanced ways in which racial prejudice continues and is ignored." —*Vogue*

"Eddo-Lodge is digesting history for those white readers who have had their ears and eyes shut to the violence in Britain's past . . . An important shift that undermines the idea that racism is the [Black, Asian, and minority ethnic] community's burden to carry.

The liberation that this book offers is in the reversal of responsibilities." —**Arifa Akbar**, *Financial Times*

"[*Why I'm No Longer Talking to White People About Race* is] deep, it's important and I suggest taking a deep breath, delving in and I promise you will come up for air woke and better equipped to understand the underlying issues of race in our society." —**Sharmaine Lovegrove**, *Elle*

"The provocative title is hard to ignore, and so is the book's cover. Seen from afar, it appears to be called *Why I'm No Longer Talking About Race*, which is intriguing enough on its own. You have to look closer to see *To White People* hiding underneath it in debossed letters. It's a striking visual representation of white people's blindness to everyday, structural racism . . . a systemic problem that needs to be tackled by those who run the system." —**NPR.org**

"*Why I'm No Longer Talking to White People About Race* by Reni Eddo-Lodge is a timely and sparky discussion about a vital subject." —*The Times Literary Supplement*, **Books of the Year**

"A book that's set to blow apart the understanding of race relations in this country." —*Stylist*

"Timely and resonant. The author's passages on intersectionality are particularly poignant. [*Why I'm No*

Longer Talking to White People About Race is] a powerful and important read, relevant and accessible whatever your race." —*The Observer,* Books of the Year

"Look[s] at racial dynamics in the UK, and does so with intelligence and poignance. Eddo-Lodge's journalism background makes the book the perfect mixture of fact and opinion, resulting in a book that will probably teach you a lot about Britain's racist history." —Cultured Vultures, 10 Best Books of the Year

"Thought-provoking (and deeply uncomfortable) . . . What Eddo-Lodge does is to force her readers to confront their own complicity . . . Her book is a call to action . . . What makes the book radical is the way it shifts the burden of ending racism on to white people." —*Sunday Herald*

"Offering extraordinary and articulate insights into contemporary race relations, *Why I'm No Longer Talking to White People About Race* is impressively informative, exceptionally well written, organized and presented, and an essential, core addition to both community and academic library Contemporary Social Issues in general, and Race Relations supplemental studies lists in particular." —*Midwest Book Review*

"A clear and convincing dissection of racism and the white denial that perpetuates it." —*Shelf Awareness,* Best Adult Books of the Year—Nonfiction

"A must-read that expertly reflects the challenges of addressing structural racism." —*Library Journal*

"A plainspoken, hard-hitting take on mainstream British society's avoidance of race and the complexities and manifestations of racism . . . Eddo-Lodge's crisp prose and impassioned voice implore white Britain to look beyond obvious racism to acknowledge the more opaque existence of structural racism . . . With this thoughtful and direct book, Eddo-Lodge stokes the very conversation that the title rejects." —*Publishers Weekly*

"In her probing and personal narrative, Eddo-Lodge offers fresh insight into the way all racism is ultimately a 'white problem' that must be addressed by commitment to action, no matter how small . . . A sharp, compelling, and impassioned book." —*Kirkus Reviews*

"This is the kind of book that demands a future where we'll no longer need such a book." —**Marlon James, Man Booker Prize–winning author of** *A Brief History of Seven Killings*

"Daring, interrogatory, illuminating. A forensic dissection of race in the UK from one of the country's most critical young thinkers. Reni's penetrative voice is like a punch to the jugular. Read it, then tell everyone you know." —**Irenosen Okojie, author of** *Butterfly Fish*

"One of the most important books of 2017." —Nikesh Shukla, editor of *The Good Immigrant*

"I've never been so excited about a book. Thank God somebody finally wrote it. Blistering. Absolutely vital writing from one of the most exciting voices in British politics. A stunningly important debut. Fellow white people: It's our responsibility to read this book. This book is essential reading for anyone even remotely interested in living in a fairer, kinder, and more equal world." —Paris Lees

"Laying bare the mechanisms by which we internalize the assumptions, false narratives, and skewed perceptions that perpetuate racism, Eddo-Lodge enables readers of every ethnicity to look at life with clearer eyes. A powerful, compelling, and urgent read." —Ann Morgan, author of *A Year of Reading the World*

WHY I'M NO LONGER TALKING TO WHITE PEOPLE ABOUT RACE

RENI EDDO-LODGE

BLOOMSBURY PUBLISHING
NEW YORK · LONDON · OXFORD · NEW DELHI · SYDNEY

BLOOMSBURY PUBLISHING
Bloomsbury Publishing Inc.
1385 Broadway, New York, NY 10018, USA

BLOOMSBURY, BLOOMSBURY PUBLISHING, and the Diana logo
are trademarks of
Bloomsbury Publishing Plc

First published in 2017 in Great Britain
First published in the United States 2017
This paperback edition published 2019

Extract on pp.158–59 from *Ain't I a Woman: Black Women and Feminism*,
by bell hooks © Gloria Jean Watkins 1981

Extract on p.101 reprinted by arrangement with The Heirs to the Estate of
Martin Luther King Jr., c/o Writers House as agent for the proprietor New York,
NY © 1963 by Martin Luther King, Jr. © renewed 1991 Coretta Scott King

For legal purposes the Acknowledgements on p. 255 constitute an
extension of this copyright page.

Parts of this book have previously been published in *New Humanist*
magazine, the *Voice*, telegraph.co.uk, openDemocracy.net, theguardian.com,
renieddolodge.co.uk, and *Inside Housing* magazine.

ISBN: HB: 978-1-4088-7055-6; eBook: 978-1-4088-7057-0;
PB: 978-1-63557-295-7

Library of Congress Cataloging-in-Publication Data is available

A catalogue record for this book is available from the British Library

2 4 6 8 10 9 7 5 3 1

Typeset by NewGen Knowledge Works (P) Ltd., Chennai, India
Printed and bound in the U.S.A. by Berryville Graphics Inc., Berryville, Virginia

To find out more about our authors and books visit
www.bloomsbury.com and sign up for our newsletters.

Bloomsbury books may be purchased for business or promotional use.
For information on bulk purchases please contact Macmillan Corporate and
Premium Sales Department at specialmarkets@macmillan.com.

For T&T

CONTENTS

PREFACE

On 22 February 2014, I published a post on my blog. I titled it 'Why I'm No Longer Talking to White People about Race'.

It read:

I'm no longer engaging with white people on the topic of race. Not all white people, just the vast majority who refuse to accept the legitimacy of structural racism and its symptoms. I can no longer engage with the gulf of an emotional disconnect that white people display when a person of colour articulates their experience. You can see their eyes shut down and harden. It's like treacle is poured into their ears, blocking up their ear canals. It's like they can no longer hear us.

This emotional disconnect is the conclusion of living a life oblivious to the fact that their skin colour is the norm and all others deviate from it. At best, white people have been taught not to mention that people of colour are 'different' in case it offends us. They truly believe that the experiences of their life as a result of their skin colour can and should be universal. I just can't engage with the bewilderment and the defensiveness as they try to grapple with the fact that not everyone experiences the world in the way that they do. They've never had to think about what it means, in power terms, to be white, so any time they're vaguely reminded of this fact, they interpret it as an affront. Their eyes glaze over in boredom or widen in indignation. Their mouths start twitching as they get defensive. Their throats open up as they try to interrupt, itching to talk over you but not really listen, because they need to let you know that you've got it wrong.

The journey towards understanding structural racism still requires people of colour to prioritise white feelings. Even if they can hear you, they're not really listening. It's like something happens to the words as they leave our mouths and reach their ears. The words hit a barrier of denial and they don't get any further.

That's the emotional disconnect. It's not really surprising, because they've never known what it means to embrace a person of colour as a true equal, with thoughts and feelings that are as valid as their own. Watching *The Color of Fear*[1] by Lee Mun Wah, I saw people of colour break down in tears as they struggled to convince a defiant white man that his words were enforcing and perpetuating a white racist standard on them. All the while he stared obliviously, completely confused by this pain, at best trivialising it, at worst ridiculing it.

I've written before about this white denial being the ubiquitous politics of race that operates on its inherent invisibility. So I can't talk to white people about race any more because of the consequent denials, awkward cartwheels and mental acrobatics that they display when this is brought to their attention. Who really wants to be alerted to a structural system that benefits them at the expense of others?

I can no longer have this conversation, because we're often coming at it from completely different places. I can't have a conversation with them about the details of a problem if they don't even recognise that the problem exists. Worse still is the white person who might be willing to entertain the possibility of said racism, but who thinks we enter this conversation as equals. We don't.

Not to mention that entering into conversation with defiant white people is a frankly dangerous task for me. As the heckles rise and the defiance grows, I have to tread incredibly carefully, because if I express frustration, anger or exasperation at their refusal to understand, they will tap into their pre-subscribed racist tropes about angry black people who are a threat to them and their safety. It's very likely that they'll then paint me as a bully or an abuser. It's also likely that their white friends will rally round them, rewrite history and make the lies the truth. Trying to engage with them and navigate their racism is not worth that.

Amid every conversation about Nice White People feeling silenced by conversations about race, there is a sort of ironic and glaring lack of understanding or empathy for those of us who have been visibly marked out as different for our entire lives, and live the consequences. It's truly a lifetime of self-censorship that people of colour have to live. The options are: speak your truth and face the reprisal, or bite your tongue and get ahead in life. It must be a strange life, always having permission to speak and feeling indignant when you're finally asked to listen. It stems from white people's never-questioned entitlement, I suppose.

I cannot continue to emotionally exhaust myself trying to get this message across, while also toeing a very precarious line that tries not to implicate any one white person in their role of perpetuating structural racism, lest they character assassinate me.

So I'm no longer talking to white people about race. I don't have a huge amount of power to change the way the world works, but I can set boundaries. I can halt the entitlement they feel towards me and I'll start that by stopping the conversation. The balance is too far swung in their favour. Their intent is often not to listen or learn, but to exert their power, to prove me wrong, to emotionally drain me, and to rebalance the status quo. I'm not talking to white people about race unless I absolutely have to. If there's something like a media or conference appearance that means that someone might hear what I'm saying and feel less alone, then I'll participate. But I'm no longer dealing with people who don't want to hear it, wish to ridicule it and, frankly, don't deserve it.

After I pressed publish, the blog post took on a life of its own. Years later, I still meet new people, in different countries and different situations, who tell me that they've read it. In 2014, as the post was being linked to all over the Internet, I braced myself for the usual slew of racist comments. But the response was markedly different, so much so that it surprised me.

There was a clear racial split in how the post was received. I got lots of messages from black and brown people. There were many 'thank you's and lots of 'you've articulated my experience'. There were reports of tears, and a little bit of debate about how to approach the problem, with education being rated highly as a solution to bridge the communication gap. Reading these messages was a relief. I knew how difficult it was to put that feeling of frustration into words, so when people got in contact and thanked me for explaining something they'd always struggled to, I was glad that it had served them. I knew that if I was feeling less alone, then they were feeling less alone too.

What I wasn't expecting was an outpouring of emotion from white people who felt that by deciding to stop talking to white people about race, I was taking something away from the world, and that this was an absolute tragedy. 'Heartbreaking' seemed to be the word that best described this sentiment.

'I'm so damn sorry you have been made to feel like this,' one commenter wrote. 'As a white person I'm painfully embarrassed by the systemic privilege we deny and enjoy on a daily basis. And painfully embarrassed that I didn't even realise it myself until about ten years ago.'

Another commenter pleaded: 'Don't stop talking to white people, your voice is clear and important, and there are ways of getting through.' Another one, this time from a black commenter, read: 'It would be such a painstaking task to persuade people, but we should not stop.' And a final, definitive comment read simply: 'Please don't give up on white people.'

Although these responses were sympathetic, they were evidence of the same communication gap I'd written about in the blog post. There seemed to be a misunderstanding of who this piece of writing was for. It was never written with the intention of prompting guilt in white people, or to provoke any kind of epiphany. I didn't know at the time that I had inadvertently written a break-up letter to whiteness. And I didn't expect white readers to do the Internet equivalent of standing outside my bedroom window with a boom box and a bunch of flowers, confessing their flaws and mistakes, begging me not to leave. This all seemed strange and slightly uncomfortable to me. Because, in writing that blog post, all I had felt I was saying was that I had had enough. It wasn't a cry for help, or a grovelling plea for white people's understanding and compassion. It wasn't an invitation for white people to indulge in self-flagellation. I stopped talking to white people about race because I don't think giving up is a sign of weakness. Sometimes it's about self-preservation.

I've turned 'Why I'm No Longer Talking to White People About Race' into a book – paradoxically – to continue the conversation. Since I set my boundary, I've done almost nothing but speak about race – at music festivals and in TV studios, to secondary-school pupils and political party conferences – and the demand for this conversation shows no signs of subsiding. People want to talk about it. This book is the product of five years of agitation, frustration, exhausting explanations, and paragraph-long Facebook comments. It's about not just the explicit side, but the slippery side of racism – the bits that are hard to define, and the bits that make you doubt yourself. Britain is still profoundly uncomfortable with race and difference.

Since I wrote that blog post in 2014, things have changed a lot for me. I now spend most of my time talking to white people about race. The publishing industry is *very* white, so there's no way I could have got this book published without talking to at least *some* white people about race. And in my research, I've had to talk to white people I never thought I'd ever exchange words with, including former British National Party leader Nick Griffin. I know a lot of people think he shouldn't be given a platform for his views to be aired unchallenged, and I agonised over the interview on page 123. I'm not the first person with a platform to give Nick Griffin airtime, but I hope I've handled his words responsibly.

A quick word on definitions. In this book, the phrase 'people of colour' is used to define anyone of any race that isn't white. I've used it because it's an infinitely better definition than simply 'non-white' – a moniker that brings with it a suggestion of something lacking, and of a deficiency. I use the word black in this book to describe people of African and Caribbean heritage, including mixed-race people. I quote a lot of research, so you will occasionally read the phrase black and minority ethnic (or BME). It's not a term I like very much, because it conjures thoughts of clinical diversity monitoring forms, but in the interests of interpreting the research as accurately as possible, I have chosen to stick to it.

I write – and read – to assure myself that other people have felt what I'm feeling too, that it isn't just me, that this is real, and valid, and true. I am only acutely aware of race because I've been rigorously marked out as different by the world I know for as long as I can remember. Although I analyse invisible whiteness and ponder its exclusionary nature often, I watch as an outsider. I understand that this isn't the case for most white people, who move through the world blissfully unaware of their own race until its dominance is called into question. When white people pick up a magazine, scroll through the Internet, read a newspaper or switch on the TV, it is never rare or odd to see people who look like them in positions of power or exerting authority. In culture particularly, the positive affirmations of whiteness are so widespread that the average white person doesn't even notice them. Instead, these affirmations are placidly consumed. To be white is to be human; to be white is universal. I only know this because I am not.

I've written this book to articulate that feeling of having your voice and confidence snatched away from you in the cocky face of the status quo. It has been written to counter the lack of the historical knowledge and the political backdrop you need to anchor your opposition to racism. I hope you use it as a tool.

I won't ever stop myself from speaking about race. Every voice raised against racism chips away at its power. We can't afford to stay silent. This book is an attempt to speak.

1

HISTORIES

It wasn't until my second year of university that I started to think about black British history. I must have been about nineteen or twenty, and I had made a new friend. We were studying the same course, and we were hanging around together because of proximity and a fear of loneliness, rather than any particular shared interests. Ticking class boxes for an upcoming term found us both opting to take a module on the transatlantic slave trade. Neither of us knew quite what to expect. I'd only ever encountered black history through American-centric educational displays and lesson plans in primary and secondary school. With a heavy focus on Rosa Parks, Harriet Tubman's Underground Railroad and Martin Luther King, Jr, the household names of America's civil rights movement felt important to me, but also a million miles away from my life as a young black girl growing up in north London.

But this short university module changed my perspective completely. It dragged Britain's colonial history and slave-trading past incredibly close to home. During

1

the course, I learnt that it was possible to jump on a train and visit a former slave port in three hours. And I did just that, taking a trip to Liverpool. Liverpool had been Britain's biggest slave port. One and a half million African people had passed through the city's ports. The Albert Dock opened four decades after Britain's final slave ship, the *Kitty's Amelia*, set sail from the city, but it was the closest I could get to staring out at the sea and imagining Britain's complicity in the slave trade. Standing on the edge of the dock, I felt despair. Walking past the city's oldest buildings, I felt sick. Everywhere I looked, I could see slavery's legacy.

At university, things were starting to slot into place for me. In a tutorial, I distinctly remember a debate about whether racism was simply discrimination, or discrimination plus power. Thinking about power made me realise that racism was about so much more than personal prejudice. It was about being in the position to negatively affect other people's life chances. My outlook began to change drastically. My friend, on the other hand, stuck around for a couple of tutorials before dropping out of the class altogether. 'It's just not for me,' she said.

Her words didn't sit well with me. Now I understand why. I resented the fact that she seemed to feel that this section of British history was in no way relevant to her. She was indifferent to the facts. Perhaps to her, the accounts didn't seem real or urgent or pertinent to the way we live now. I don't know what she thought, because I didn't have the vocabulary to raise it with her at the time. But I know now that I was resentful of her because I felt that her whiteness allowed her to be disinterested in Britain's violent history, to close her eyes and walk away. To me, this didn't seem like information you could opt out from learning.

With the rapid advancement in technology transforming how we live – leaps and bounds being taken in just decades rather than centuries – the past has never felt so distant. In this context, it's easy to view slavery as something Terrible, that happened A Very Long Time Ago. It's easy to convince yourself that the past has no bearing on how we live today. But the Abolition of Slavery Act was introduced in the British Empire in 1833, less than two hundred years ago. Given that the British began trading in African slaves in 1562, slavery as a British institution existed for much longer than it has currently been abolished – over 270 years. Generation after generation of black lives stolen, families torn apart, communities split. Thousands of people being born into slavery and dying enslaved, never knowing what it might mean to be free. Entire lives sustaining constant brutality and violence, living in never-ending fear. Generation after generation of white wealth amassed from the profits of slavery, compounded, seeping into the fabric of British society.

Slavery was an international trade. White Europeans, including the British, bartered with African elites, exchanging products and goods for African people, what some white slave traders called 'black cattle'. Over the course of the slave trade, an estimated 11,000,000 black African people were transported across the Atlantic Ocean to work unpaid on sugar and cotton plantations in the Americas and West Indies.

The records kept were not dissimilar to the accounts of a modern-day business, as they documented profit and loss, and itemised lists of black people purchased and sold. This human livestock – these 'black cattle' – was the ideal commodity. Slaves were lucrative stock. Black women's reproductive systems were industrialised. Children born into slavery were the default property of slave owners, and this meant limitless labour at no extra cost. That reproduction was made all the easier by the routine rape of African women slaves by white slave owners.

Profit and loss also meant documenting the deaths of 'black cattle', because it was bad for business. The vast slave ships that transported African people across the Atlantic were severely cramped. The journey could take up to three months. The space around each slave was coffin-like, consigning them to live among filth and bodily fluids. The dead and dying

4

were thrown overboard for cash-flow reasons: insurance money could be collected for those slaves that died at sea.

The image of the slave ship *Brooks*, first published in 1788 by abolitionist William Elford, depicted typical conditions.[1] It shows a well-packed slave ship: bodies are lined up one by one, horizontally in four rows (with three short extra rows at the back of the ship), illustrating the callous efficiency used to transport a cargo of African people. The *Brooks* was owned by a Liverpudlian merchant named Joseph Brooks.

But slavery wasn't just happening in Liverpool. Bristol, too, had a slave port, as well as Lancaster, Exeter, Plymouth, Bridport, Chester, Lancashire's Poulton-le-Fylde and, of course, London.[2] Although enslaved African people moved through British shores regularly, the plantations they toiled on were not in Britain, but rather in Britain's colonies. The majority were in the Caribbean, so, unlike the situation in America, most British people saw the money without the blood. Some British people owned plantations that ran almost entirely on slave labour. Others bought just a handful of plantation slaves, with the intention of getting a return on their investment. Many Scottish men went to work as slave drivers in Jamaica, and some brought their slaves with them when they moved back to Britain. Slaves, like any other personal property, could be inherited, and many Brits lived comfortably off the toil of enslaved black people without being directly involved in the transaction.

The Society for Effecting the Abolition of the Slave Trade, which was founded in London in 1787, was the idea of civil servant Granville Sharp and campaigner Thomas Clarkson. Sharp and Clarkson formed the society with ten other men, most of whom were Quakers. They campaigned for forty-seven years, generating broad-based support and attracting high-profile leadership from Members of Parliament – the most famous being abolitionist William Wilberforce. The public pressure of the campaign was successful, and an Act of Parliament declared slavery abolished in the British Empire in 1833. But the recipients of the compensation for the dissolution of a significant money-making industry were not those who had been enslaved. Instead it was the 46,000 British slave-owning citizens who received cheques for their financial losses.[3] Such one-sided compensation seemed to be the logical conclusion for a country that had traded in human flesh.

Despite abolition, an Act of Parliament was not going to change the perception overnight of enslaved African people from quasi-animal to human. Less than two hundred years later, that damage is still to be undone.

After university, I was hungry for more information. I wanted to know about black people in Britain, post-slavery. However, this information was not easily accessible. This was history only available to people who truly cared, only knowable through a hefty amount of self-directed study. So I actively sought it out, and I began by looking into Black History Month.

The existence of Black History Month in the UK is relatively recent. It wasn't until 1987 that local authorities in London began putting on events to celebrate black contributions to Britain. Linda Bellos was born in London to a Nigerian father and a white British mother, and it was under her leadership that a British Black History Month came to exist. At the time, she was leader of south London's Lambeth Council and chair of the London Strategic Policy Unit (part of the now defunct Greater London Council). The idea for Black History Month was put to her by Ansel Wong, chief officer of the Strategic Policy Unit's race equality division. 'I said yes, let's do it,' she explained to me from her home in Norwich.

'I thought Black History Month was a great idea. What I wasn't going to do was make it like the American one, because we have a different history . . . There's so many people who have no idea – and I'm talking about white people – no idea about the history of racism. They don't know why we're in this country.'

Ansel organised the first Black History Month, and Linda hosted the event. It was a London-wide affair. The decision to hold it in October was largely logistical, the United States have held their Black History Month in February since it began in 1970. 'Our guest of honour was Sally Mugabe,' Linda explained. 'It was insufficient time to invite [her]. If we'd done it two weeks [later], then we wouldn't have got the people we needed.

'We were more inclusive,' she added. 'Black was defined in its political terms. African and Asian.[4] We only ran it for two years, because Thatcher was cutting all our budgets. It would have been an indulgence.'

After two years of central funding and leadership from the London Strategic Policy Unit dried up, Black History Month continued in Britain, albeit sporadically. Today, Black History Month is firmly established in Britain, and has been running for thirty years. It tends to consist of exhibitions of work from artists from the African diaspora, panel events debating race, and softer cultural celebrations, like fashion shows and food festivals. Speaking to Linda, it felt like she was sceptical of the values of current-day Black History Month activities. When I asked her why she wanted Black History Month in Britain, she said it was to 'celebrate the contribution that black people had made in the United Kingdom. It wasn't about hair . . . it was history month, not culture month. There had been a history, a history that I had been aware of, from my own father's experience.'

The history of blackness in Britain has been a piece-meal one. For an embarrassingly long time, I didn't even realise that black people had been slaves in Britain. There was a received wisdom that all black and brown people in the UK were recent immigrants, with little discussion of the history of colonialism, or of *why* people from Africa and Asia came to settle in Britain. I knew vaguely of the Windrush Generation, the 492 Caribbeans who travelled to Britain by boat in 1948. This was because they were the older relatives of people I knew at school. There was no 'black presence in Britain' presentation that didn't include the *Windrush*. But most of my knowledge of black history was American history. This was an inadequate education in a country where increasing generations of black and brown people continue to consider themselves British (including me). I had been denied a context, an ability to understand myself. I needed to know why, when people waved Union Jacks and shouted 'we want our country back', it felt like the chant was aimed at people like me. What history had I inherited that left me an alien in my place of birth?

On 1 November 2008, at an event marking the fiftieth anniversary of the Institute of Race Relations, the institute's director Ambalavaner Sivanandan told his audience: 'we are here because you were there'. That phrase has since been absorbed into black British vocabulary. Wanting to know more about what it meant, I reached back, searching for evidence. The first answer I found was war.

Britain's involvement in the First World War wasn't just limited to British citizens. Thanks to its rabid empire building, people from countries that weren't European (apart from colonisation), were caught up in the expectation of dying for King and Country. When, in 2013, the British Council asked people about their perceptions of the First World War, they found that most Brits didn't have an understanding of the international impact it had, despite the moniker 'world war'. 'Because of the reach of empires,' the council's report reads, 'soldiers and labourers were enlisted from all over the globe.'[5] Of the seven countries[6] the British Council surveyed on the First World War, the vast majority of respondents thought that both western and eastern Europe were involved. In comparison, an average of just 17 per cent thought that Asia was involved, and just 11 per cent of respondents identified Africa's involvement.

It could be that this misconception about exactly who fought for Britain during the First World War has led to a near erasure of the contributions of black and brown people. This is an erasure that couldn't be further from the truth. Over a million Indian soldiers – or sepoys (Indian soldiers serving for Britain) – fought for Britain during the First World War.[7] Britain had promised these soldiers that their country would be free from colonial rule if they did so. Sepoys travelled to Britain in the belief that they would not only be fighting for Britain, but by doing so they would be contributing to their country's eventual freedom.

Their journey to Europe was unforgiving. They travelled by ship, without the appropriate clothing for the shift in climate. Many sepoys suffered from a bitter cold that they'd never before experienced, with some dying from exposure. And even during the war, sepoys didn't receive the treatment they were expecting. The highest-ranking sepoy was still lower in the army hierarchy than the lowest-ranking white British soldier. If injured, a sepoy would be treated in the segregated Brighton Pavilion and Dome Hospital for Indian Troops. The hospital was surrounded with barbed wire to discourage wounded sepoys from mixing with the locals. Around 74,000 sepoys died fighting in the war, but Britain refused to deliver its promise of releasing India from colonial rule.

A much smaller number of soldiers travelled from the West Indies to fight for Britain.[8] The Memorial Gates Trust, a charity set up to commemorate Indian, African and Caribbean soldiers who died for Britain in both world wars, puts the number at 15,600. These soldiers were known as the British West Indies Regiment (BWIR). In the Caribbean, the British Army recruited from poor areas, and, similarly to India, there was a feeling among some would-be recruits that taking part in the war would lead to political reform at home. But this opinion wasn't widespread, and there were a significant number of Caribbean people who were set against the West Indies fighting, calling it a 'white man's war'. Despite the resistance of some, thousands of West Indians quit their jobs to travel to Europe.

Again, the long boat journey was unforgiving. Britain needed the extra labour, yet the government failed to provide West Indians with adequate clothing to survive the journey, just as they had with the sepoys. In 1916, the SS *Verdala*, travelling from the West Indies to West Sussex, had to make a diversion to Halifax in eastern Canada. Hundreds of West Indian recruits suffered from frostbite, with some dying from exposure to the harsh, cold climate.

When they arrived, the majority of the British West Indies Regiment did not initially fight alongside white British soldiers on the battlefield. Instead, they were relegated to supporting positions, doing drudgework for the benefit of white soldiers. Their duties included strenuous labour, such as digging trenches, building roads, and carrying injured soldiers on stretchers. As white British ranks were depleted in battle, West Indian soldiers were given permission to fight. Almost two hundred men had died in action by the end of the war.

By 1918, resentment among West Indian soldiers was widespread. While the BWIR was stationed in

Taranto, Italy, some men got hold of news that white British soldiers had received a pay rise that the West Indian soldiers had been excluded from. Outraged at their treatment, the soldiers went on strike, gathering signatures for a petition to be sent to the Secretary of State. This quickly evolved into an open rebellion. During the Taranto mutiny, a striker was shot dead by a black non-commissioned officer, and a bomb was set off. The rebellion was quickly crushed and sixty suspected rebellious members of the British West Indies Regiment were tried for their involvement in mutiny. Some were jailed, and one man was sentenced to death by firing squad.

Mistreated West Indian soldiers returned home, and the crackdown on the Taranto mutiny contributed to a push for a black self-determination movement in the Caribbean. But there were also black soldiers who chose to stay on in Britain after the war. As the fighting came to an end and soldiers were demobilised, black ex-soldiers living in Britain began to be targeted.

Riots always seem to kick off in the summer. On 6 June 1919, seven months after the First World War had ended, rumours were doing the rounds in Newport, south Wales. It was alleged that a white woman had been slighted by a black man. As increasing numbers of angry and agitated white people shared the news among themselves, a braying mob assembled and then descended on homes of black men in the area. Some of the black men shot back with guns. Fights and scuffles over the next few days led to a Caribbean man stabbing a white man.

Just five days later, on 11 June, the *South Wales Echo* reported: 'a brake [vehicle] containing a number of coloured men and white women was going along East Canal Wharf. It attracted a crowd.'[9] Cardiff, another port city, had been whipped up in anti-black sentiment. On seeing these black men and white women together, a frenzied mob of white people began throwing rocks at the vehicle. It's not clear if anyone in the vehicle was injured. Days later, in violent protest at the audacity of interracial relationships, another angry crowd of white people set upon a lone white woman, who was known to have married an African man. They stripped her naked.

In the port city of Liverpool, similar race hatred was gaining ground. Post-war employment was scarce, and over a hundred black factory workers suddenly and swiftly lost their jobs after white workers refused to work with them. On 4 June 1919, a Caribbean man was stabbed in the face by two white men after an argument over a cigarette. Numerous fights followed, with the police ransacking homes where they knew black people lived. The frenzy resulted in one of the most horrific race hate crimes in British history.

Twenty-four-year-old black seaman Charles Wootton was accosted by an enraged white crowd and thrown into the King's Dock. As he swam, desperately trying to lift himself out of the water, he was pelted with bricks until he sank under the surface. Some time later, his lifeless body was dragged out of the dock. It was a public lynching. The days after Charles Wootton's murder saw white mob rule dominating Liverpool's streets as they attacked any black person they saw.[10]

These acts of vicious race hatred did not go unseen by the British government. Concerned by the levels of unrest across the country, the state responded in the only way it knew how – a repatriation drive. As a result, six hundred black people were sent 'back to where they came from' by September 1919.[11]

Despite its best efforts to pretend otherwise, Britain is far from a monoculture. Outward-facing when it suited best, history shows us that this country had created a global empire it could draw labour from at ease. But it wasn't ready for the repercussions and responsibilities that came with its colonising of countries and cultures. It was black and brown people who suffered the consequences.

But some of those people fought back. Born in 1882 in Kingston, Jamaica, Dr Harold Moody was not one of the young Caribbeans who fought for Britain in the First World War. Instead, he arrived in Bristol in 1904, aged twenty-two, with a focus on advancing his education. He had his heart set on becoming a doctor, and had spent time working at his father's successful pharmacy business in Kingston to save up the funds for his studies. With Jamaica still under British rule, his move to England wasn't a surprise; among Jamaicans, Britain was seen as the 'Mother Country'.

Upon his arrival, he boarded an express train to London Paddington and took himself to a hostel – the Young Men's Christian Association, now known as the YMCA – until he found somewhere more permanent to live. It was during these first days on British soil that he learned the mother country wasn't going to be as hospitable as he'd been led to believe. He struggled to rent, and was turned away from a number of potential lodgings before managing to find a place in Canonbury, north London.

Once settled, Harold began medical training. He graduated in 1912 and set about looking for a job. He applied for a position at King's College Hospital, but his potential employers did not want to hire a black man.[12] He tried again, applying for a position in south London, with the Camberwell Board of Guardians. The board was part of Camberwell's Poor Law Parish, a local government organisation that oversaw the well-being of the area's most elderly and vulnerable residents with an infirmary, as well as managing children's homes and workhouses. He was turned away from this job too, but not before being told 'the poor people would not have a nigger attend to them'.[13] Determined to serve the community, Harold responded to these knock-backs by setting up his own private practice.

A year after qualifying, Dr Moody's practice opened at 111 King's Road in Peckham, south-east London. Although he'd faced overt acts of racist discrimination, it was his Christianity rather than his politics that drew Dr Moody to his activism. For him, racism was a religious issue. He was active in the wider Christian community. His respectable, middle-class job positioned him as a beacon for black people in 1920s and 1930s Britain. He advocated on their behalf, quickly becoming known as a man who would help if you were in need. That popularity and momentum led Dr Harold Moody to form the League of Coloured Peoples in 1931.

The League was both a Christian mission and a campaigning organisation. Its objectives, published in its quarterly journal *The Keys*, were:

- To promote and protect the social, educational, economic and political interests of its members
- To interest members in the welfare of coloured peoples in all parts of the world
- To improve relations between the races
- To cooperate and affiliate with organisations sympathetic to coloured people[14]

First published in 1933, *The Keys* served as the written arm of the League, campaigning against racism in employment, housing and wider society. In 1937, *The Keys* published a sternly worded exchange with the Manchester Hospital about the barring of black nurses' employment. The letter questioned a quote from the hospital's Matron L. G. Duff Grant, who had written, quite openly, 'we have never taken coloured nurses for training here. The question was once raised at Nursing Committee, and there was a definite rule that no one of negroid extraction can be considered.' Dr Moody, then President of the League, wrote to the hospital's board, only to find that no such rule was in place. 'There is', read the reply from N. Cobboth, chair of the board, 'no rule against the admission of coloured women for training as nurses at the Manchester Royal Infirmary and the Board wish it to be understood that each individual application will be considered on its merits.'[15]

Dr Moody's work with the League of Coloured Peoples was quite possibly Britain's first anti-racism campaign in the twentieth century, and it would have far-reaching implications for Britain's race relations in the future.

As Dr Harold Moody was doing pioneering work for black people while he was based in London, an aspect of his personal life – his relationship with a white woman and their mixed-race children[16] – was seen as a point of great contention in British society at that time. Mixed-race relationships were controversial in the early twentieth century, and in the north-west of England these relationships were considered disturbing enough to justify academic research. In the late 1920s, the University of Liverpool was solidifying its social sciences department, headed up by anthropologist Rachel M. Fleming. Her research was on what she called 'hybrid children' – those with black fathers and white mothers.[17] With Liverpool being a port city, there were plenty of black seamen who had taken up permanent residence. Academics estimate that Liverpool's black population was five thousand at the time. Against the backdrop of race-fuelled riots and the lynching of Charles Wootton, mixed-race relationships did exist, but were seen by many as a social problem that needed to be stamped out.

It was in this context that Rachel Fleming won the support of Liverpool's authority figures to research Liverpool's 'wretched' – read: mixed-race – children. She founded the Liverpool Association for the Welfare of Half-Caste Children in 1927. Muriel Fletcher, a University of Liverpool graduate working as a probation officer, was tasked with writing the association's first report. Her work meant that through welfare services she had contact with some of the poorest families in the city, and it was through this skewed lens with some of Liverpool's poorest mixed-race families that she conducted her research.

The *Report on an Investigation into the Colour Problem in Liverpool and Other Ports* was published in June 1930. It concluded, with scant evidence, that venereal diseases were twice as likely to be found in black seamen than white seamen, and that mixed-race – or to use the language of the report, 'half-caste' – children were more likely to be sickly because of this. 'The children seemed to have frequent colds, many were also rickety, and several cases were reported in which there was a bad family history for tuberculosis,' wrote Ms Fletcher. Perhaps reflecting popular attitudes at the time, Fletcher deemed mixed-race girls and women as tainted by their race, writing 'only two cases have been found in Liverpool of half-caste girls who have married white men, and in one of these cases the girl's family forced the marriage on the man.'[18] In her report, Muriel Fletcher organised the white women who chose to have relationships with black men into four categories: the mentally weak, the prostitutes, the young and reckless, and those who felt forced into marriage because of illegitimate children.

Children who were researched in the study had their eyes examined and their noses measured, with their facial features categorised as either 'Negroid' or 'English'. Commenting on the fact that mixed-race young adults struggled to find work, Fletcher wrote: 'mothers of a better type regretted the fact that they had brought these children into the world, handicapped by their colour.' Echoing the hugely popular eugenics movement at the time, it seems that Muriel Fletcher thought that race mixing – or, as eugenicists called it, miscegenation – was such an abomination that the children of mixed-race relationships had 'little future'.

Popular at the beginning of the twentieth century, the British eugenics movement believed that social class was determined by biological factors such as intelligence, health and the vague criteria of 'moral values'. Eugenicists argued that those with desirable qualities should be encouraged to reproduce, while those without should be discouraged. The racism was inherent here: whiteness was to be aspired to, whereas any hint of black heritage was considered a kind of contamination, leading to a hard line against mixed-race relationships and mixed-race people. Despite support from influential names like John Maynard Keynes and George Bernard Shaw, there was no legislation passed in Britain to cement eugenics into the workings of the state (for example, forced sterilisation), and a 1931 Private Members Bill advocating this was outvoted in Parliament.

On publication, Muriel Fletcher's *Report on an Investigation into the Colour Problem in Liverpool and Other Ports* had a national impact, with a representative of the Anti-Slavery Society calling it an 'extraordinarily able document' containing 'the most impressive and authoritative detail'. In a recent study on the report, academic Mark Christian argued that it had a long-lasting negative effect on the black people of Liverpool, and cemented the use of the term 'half-caste'.[19]

The aftermath of yet another world war brought with it fresh labour demands, and Britain once again encouraged immigration. When the SS *Empire Windrush* sailed from the Caribbean to England, it carried 490 Caribbean men and two Caribbean women, all of whom were prepared to muck in with the job of restoring a post-war Britain.[20] The *Windrush* docked at Tilbury in Thurrock, Essex on 22 June 1948. That same year, the government introduced the British Nationality Act – a law that effectively gave Commonwealth citizens the same rights to reside as British subjects.

The country's black population continued to rise. Between 1951 and 1961, the Caribbean-born British population grew from 15,000 to 172,000,[21] with the majority of those people from Jamaica (an increase in population from 6,000 to 100,000[22]).

By 1958, Nottingham's black population numbered 2,500. But a decade of legislation explicitly welcoming Commonwealth citizens to Britain had not changed attitudes on the ground. Quotes from a local newspaper reported a colour bar in Nottingham's pubs, with black men expected to stand aside until white people had been served. White resentment towards the city's black residents was rife, and black resentment at white resentment was simmering. On 23 August 1958, an altercation in a pub between a white woman and a black man spiralled out of control. Reports on what sparked the following events are sketchy. What we do know is this: later that day, a thousand people had crowded into St Ann's Well Road ready to riot. Razors, knives and bottles were used as weapons, and eight people were hospitalised.

What happened in Nottingham was also occurring in other parts of the country. On 20 August in Notting Hill, west London, a group of teddy boys – young rock-and-roll-loving white men who wore creeper shoes and suits – set upon the streets with the sole objective of attacking black people. They called themselves the 'nigger hunters'. That night, their violent spree put five black men in hospital.[23]

At the time, Notting Hill was a poor and overcrowded area of London, with desperation for housing exploited by the notorious slum landlord, Peter Rachman. Rachman's reputation was so poor that his name became a synonym for bad treatment of tenants. *Chambers 21st Century Dictionary* defines Rachmanism today as 'exploitation or extortion by a landlord of tenants living in slum conditions'.[24] It was black people who fell prey to Rachman's small dilapidated properties and extortionate rents. They had very little choice. Oral histories from those who lived through these times report 'no blacks, no dogs, no Irish' signs in the windows of other, more respectable properties.[25] This only exacerbated poor race relations in the capital.

Nine days after the nigger-hunting spree from Notting Hill's teddy boys, and a mixed-race married couple – a black man and white Swedish woman – were arguing outside Latimer Road tube station. It was an August bank holiday. With many off work, the argument drew a crowd of white men, who jumped in to defend the woman, perhaps believing that she was under attack. Spotting the onslaught, some black men got involved to support her husband. They began fighting each other.

Later, interviews with white rioters suggest that there was a rumour going around that a black man had raped a white woman.[26] This scuffle outside a train station quickly escalated into two hundred white people roaming the streets chanting racist abuse. As the fighting intensified, some white rioters berated the police for holding them back from attacking black people. The riots stretched on for three whole days.

Swastikas were painted on to the doors of black families. Black people fought back with weapons and makeshift Molotov cocktails. Those black people who were stopped on the street by the police during the violence stressed their need to defend themselves. No fatalities were recorded, but over a hundred people – the majority of them white – were arrested.

In 2002, prematurely released government files revealed that police detectives had successfully convinced then Home Secretary Rab Butler that the Notting Hill riots weren't about race, but instead were simply the work of hooligans. 'Whereas there certainly was some ill feeling between white and coloured residents in this area,' wrote Detective Sergeant M. Walters, 'it is abundantly clear much of the trouble was caused by ruffians, both coloured and white, who seized on this opportunity to indulge in hooliganism.' No mention was made of the nigger-hunting teddy boys.[27]

After Nottingham and Notting Hill, race relations in Britain were rapidly deteriorating. It was becoming clear to post-*Windrush* black people in Britain that they would not be allowed to live quietly, to work, pay tax and assimilate. That instead they would be punished for their very existence in Britain. Black and brown labour had proved integral to Britain's success in both world wars, but black people themselves would face extreme rejection in the decades that followed.

Throughout the 1950s, the government was reluctant to recognise that the country had a problem with racism. But there was some movement. In 1960, backbench Labour MP Archibald Fenner Brockway repeatedly tried to bring forward a Race Discrimination Bill with the aim of outlawing 'discrimination to the detriment of any person on the grounds of colour, race and religion in the United Kingdom'.[28] Every single one of the nine times he tabled the Bill, it was defeated.[29] On the other end of the spectrum, in 1959, Oswald Mosley, founder of the British Union of Fascists, saw fit to return to parliamentary politics after stepping down in 1930. He stood in a constituency near Notting Hill and advocated the repatriation of immigrants, losing with an 8.1 per cent share of the vote.

It wasn't until less than a decade after both the Nottingham and Notting Hill race riots that the state attempted to pose a solution to Britain's racism problem. Coming into effect on 31 May 1962, the Commonwealth Immigrants Act drastically restricted immigration rights to Britain's Commonwealth citizens. Even the wording was different. The 1948 British Nationality Act used the words 'citizens' to describe those from Commonwealth countries; in 1962 they were described as 'immigrants', adding a new layer of alien to people who had enjoyed the right to reside just fourteen years earlier. With a new emphasis on skilled workers, the Commonwealth Immigrants Act stated that those wishing to move to Britain now needed a work permit to settle in the country.[30] The logic behind this still prevails today.

Then, in 1965, Britain's first-ever race-relations legislation was granted by parliament. The Race Relations Act was an odd move for the British government, having made such a strong statement against the free movement of its Commonwealth citizens just three years earlier. The Act stated that overt racial discrimination was no longer legal in public places – although it didn't apply to shops or private housing. At the time, the BBC reported those specific acts of discrimination included 'refusing to serve a person, an unreasonable delay in serving someone, or overcharging'.[31] A Race Relations Board was created as part of the Act.[32] Its purpose was to receive complaints of, and monitor, racist incidents – no mean feat, when the 1961 census had put the general population at 52,700,000.[33] There was no way of knowing the exact number of non-white people living in Britain as the census didn't include a question on race until 1991. Barely any complaints were made to the board, and those that were made were almost futile. It had no authority to punish those against whom complaints were made. Instead, its role was one of mediation between the complainant and the organisation or person being complained about.

Britain's first race-relations act was tepid. It didn't tackle endemic housing discrimination, and it had enough caveats to allow wriggle room for those who were intent on keeping black people in Britain as second-class citizens. An inadequate antidote to decades of targeted violence and harassment, the Race Relations Board appeared to exist only for posturing reasons. Most black and Asian people in Britain didn't even know it existed. The 1965 Act's weaknesses were obvious. The efforts to challenge racism came from the very same state that had sanctioned racism decades earlier with repatriation drives in the face of racist riots – the same state that picked up and disposed of black and brown bodies at its own convenience.

The Act was strengthened three years later, outlawing the denial of housing, employment or public services on the grounds of race. However, government services were exempt from legal challenges. At the time, the BBC reported: 'The new Race Relations Act is intended to counter-balance the Immigration Act, and so fulfil the government's promise to be "fair but tough" on immigrants.'[34]

On 7 March 1965, African Americans were beaten bloody on a civil rights march led by Martin Luther King, Jr. They were demanding their constitutional right to vote. Two years before that now iconic day, in the west of England, nineteen-year-old Jamaican Guy Bailey made his way to a job interview with Bristol

Omnibus Company, the city's bus service. Paul Stephenson, a local youth worker, had arranged the interview for Guy, first ensuring that there were jobs available, and that Guy had the qualifications to do the work. But when Guy turned up to his interview, he found that it had been cancelled.

Recounting his interview to the BBC[35] fifty years later, Guy recalled the exact moment he was rejected by the receptionist. 'She said to the manager "your two o'clock appointment is here. But he's black." And the manager said, "Tell him we have no vacancies here, all vacancies are filled."'

That Guy was turned down was not a surprise to Bristol's 3,000-strong black community, the majority of whom had settled in Britain from the Caribbean after the Second World War. For them, racism in the bus service was a long-held suspicion; many had interviewed with Bristol Omnibus Company only to be turned down. Everyone who worked at the bus company was white.

But Guy Bailey's interview wasn't a coincidence. It had been set up by a small group of young men: Roy Hackett, Owen Henry, Audley Evans and Prince Brown. The group called themselves the West Indian Development Council. They asked Paul Stephenson to work with them on their plan, and he agreed. Paul already knew Guy, who was a student at the night school he taught at. Guy was a good interview prospect. He was clean cut, already employed, studying part-time, and active in a Christian youth organisation.

As soon as Guy was refused an interview, the group arranged a press conference. Local reporters crowded into Paul's flat to hear exactly what had happened. A photo shoot was arranged, with Owen echoing Rosa Parks by sitting at the back of a bus. As both local and national press reported on the case, pressure mounted on the bus service's general manager, Ian Patey. When the *Bristol Evening Post* pressed him, he said: 'You won't get a white man in London to admit it, but which of them will join a service where they may find themselves working under a coloured foreman?'[36]

Paul and the West Indian Development Council won the support of local students, saw speeches in favour of their cause from politicians, and earned sympathetic editorials in the local press. But Paul was also repeatedly ignored by the bus company and the Transport and General Workers' Union (TGWU). Though often divided by work disputes, both management and the trade union found themselves united by racism. They had an agreement, the kind that lent itself well to discrimination: the bus company was not to hire anyone not already approved by the local TGWU branch. Even though Ian Patey's comments were on

the record, Bristol Omnibus Company deflected accountability, instead passing it along to the union. Racism had
infected worker solidarity, with a union representative
at the time insisting that more black workers would be
taking away jobs for prospective white employees, and
that employing them would mean reduced hours for
current employees.

As the campaign continued, Paul was harshly criticised. Ron Nethercott, South-West Regional Secretary
of the union, wrote an article in a national newspaper
calling Paul 'dishonest' and 'irresponsible'. For his critics, it was his activism that was the root of the problem,
not the colour bar. Some of these statements led to a
libel case, which Paul won. Meanwhile, every single one
of the city's West Indian residents were boycotting the
bus service. One campaign leader told the local newspaper, 'Although it is hard to tell, many white people
are supporting us.' The campaign drew support from
Trinidad's High Commissioner Sir Learie Constantine.
Over a hundred university students marched in support, and everyone boycotting the bus service either
walked or cycled to get around the city.

The day before Martin Luther King, Jr told an audience of 250,000 that he had a dream, a meeting of five
hundred bus employees met and agreed to discontinue
Bristol Omnibus Company's unofficial colour bar. The
day after, general manager Ian Patey committed to

ending it for good. Speaking at a press conference, he announced 'the only criterion will be the person's suitability for the job'. But it is important to note that, to date, Bristol Omnibus, now merged with other companies and eventually renamed First Somerset & Avon, has never apologised for its actions. Neither has the Bristol branch of the Transport and General Workers' Union, since merged with Unite the Union.

I first learnt of the Bristol bus boycott as a graduate in 2013, when I was working at the race equality think tank the Runnymede Trust. A small team of us travelled to Bristol to launch a campaign. As well as running a pop-up 'come and talk about racism' shop, we also held evening events around the city centre. One of those events was with Paul Stephenson. By then, he was in his late seventies. Upstairs in the event space of Foyles bookshop, Paul, his voice withered by age and activism and righteous rage, commanded the attention of the whole room. I felt like I was listening to history.

Around the same time as Bristolians were organising themselves against a colour bar, white nationalist activity in Britain was gaining ground. The National Front, a whites only, anti-immigration and far-right political party, was stoking anger and resentment among British people. Formed in 1967, the National

Front has close links to white supremacist movements globally. At the height of their growth in the 1970s, party members adorned themselves with Union Jacks and St George's flags, as though they felt their politics represented the epitome of Britishness. Just over a decade after its formation, the National Front stood over three hundred people in the 1979 general election, and won almost 200,000 votes. Despite the growing popularity of white nationalist politics in Britain during the 1970s, it was black and Asian people who were considered volatile members of society. The National Front's membership eventually dwindled by the 1980s, but the sentiment of the party found its home in other forms of activism.

In the 1970s, police officers often wielded a section of the then archaic 1824 Vagrancy Act. The section in question gave the police the power to stop, search and arrest anyone they suspected might commit a crime. This Vagrancy Act came to be known as 'sus laws' (taken from wording of the Act that described a 'suspected person'). Because the police didn't keep statistics on those they were stopping under the Act, it's difficult to know just how many people were bothered by the police for the crime of not looking respectable.[37] Anecdotally, anti-racism campaigners insisted that black people were being unfairly targeted by sus laws. The notion of who does and who doesn't look suspicious – particularly in a British political climate that just ten years earlier was denying black people employment and housing – was undoubtedly racialised.

Sus laws ensured a fraught relationship between black people and the police. This was intensified by public panic about mugging and muggers. In 1972, a violent and fatal street robbery in Handsworth, Birmingham led to near constant press coverage of street robberies for the following year. 'Mugging' was an American term, imported from police statements and press coverage in black-concentrated cities. The fear of mugging was imported, too.

Street robberies have always existed in Britain. But the importation of the word mugging brought with it a coded implication that the perpetrators were overwhelmingly black, and that mugging was an exclusively black crime. Newspapers reported that it was a new trend. The fear of mugging was about so much more than the fear of crime and violence; it was about the anxieties of those who had been scared of black liberation struggles in the 1960s, and their intense fears around race, reparations and revenge.

There was at least one documented incident of police officers arresting black boys for the crime of looking like criminals. On 16 March 1972, at Oval train station in south London, a group of plain-clothes

white police officers targeted and tackled four young
black men – who also happened to be members of a
radical black organisation – on public transport, later
testifying in court that 'it was clear they intended to
pick the pockets of passengers'. But the only witnesses
for the prosecution were the police themselves, and the
accused young men had no stolen property on them.[38]
The Oval 4 were imprisoned for two years each, but
were released a year early on appeal. Every single one
of them maintained their innocence.

While the police were busy arresting black people
for looking suspicious, the National Front were
capitalising on national anti-black feeling. In 1975
they organised a march against black muggings, which
they led through London's East End. A year later,
they found another white-power cause to support.
Leamington Spa bus driver Robert Relf became a
national news story in 1976 when he put up a sign
outside of his house that read 'For sale to an English
family only'. A previous version of the sign was even
more extreme: 'To avoid animosity all round positively
no coloureds'. The sign contravened the Race Relations
Act, and he was asked to take it down. He refused and
was imprisoned for contempt of court. Relf promptly
went on hunger strike. The tabloid press used his
imprisonment as ammunition to argue against what
they called 'political correctness'. Meanwhile, for the
National Front, his were the actions of a martyr. They

launched a campaign in support of him, and organised 'Free Relf' protests.

Ideas of blackness and criminality were becoming inherently interlinked. In 1984, three years after sus laws were scrapped, stop and search was introduced. The initiatives seemed barely different. But while sus laws allowed the police to arrest anyone they thought was loitering with intent to commit a crime, the new laws meant police had to have reasonable belief that an offence had already been committed before stopping and searching a suspect.[39] While the police line has always been that such tactics prevent crime, black people have always been disproportionately targeted under stop and search (research in 2015 revealed parts of the country where black people were seventeen times more likely to be stopped and searched than white people.)[40] These were (and still are) sus laws by a different name.

Between 1980 and 1982, with the country in recession, unemployment for black and Asian men rose by roughly 20 per cent – in comparison to a rise of just 2 per cent for white men.[41] Despite black and Asian people becoming a firm fixture of the British urban landscape, some white communities were still uneasy about their presence. There was a feeling among some that unemployed young black people chose not to work, and instead took up lives of social aggravation. In a radio documentary broadcast on BRMB Radio Birmingham in 1982, PC Dick Board, a police officer working in the city, made his feelings about unemployed young black people clear. 'Let's be fair,' he said. 'We're talking about a certain type of people now. We had all these reasons in the twenties and thirties, and we never had this. We never had the soaring crime rates, and what we now know as the American phrase "mugging". Which is robbery with violence. We have a different sort of person, who by hook or by crook is going to get his own way at the expense of everybody else. Even his own kind. That's the point. Never mind this unemployment business, we've got a situation here now that is being used deliberately and there's no question about it, they couldn't care less whether they've got a job or not, in fact they're happier without them.' He continued: 'All this is complete twaddle about they're looking for jobs and "I can't get a job" and all this . . . A lot of them use their colour as leverage against us . . . they use it, and they use it very well. There's enough people in this country prepared to listen, and turn a blind eye to what these people do.'[42]

When PC Dick Board spoke about 'what these people do', I think he was referring to crime. Alongside recession-fuelled unemployment came heightened fears of crime in inner cities that stigmatised entire areas where black and brown people lived.

The summer of 1981 saw more riots across the country – in Brixton, on 10 April, in Toxteth, Liverpool on 3 July, Handsworth, Birmingham on 10 July, and Chapeltown, Leeds, in the same month. The social conditions of each area were very similar. Poor. Black. In both Brixton and Toxteth, police behaviour was a contributing factor. Brixton, the first riot of the year, was sparked by the Metropolitan Police's Operation Swamp, in which they performed over a thousand stop and searches in just six days.[43] When police officers stopped to help a wounded black boy, a crowd approached them, and the situation escalated.[44] In Toxteth, the police gave chase to a black motorcyclist, believing his vehicle was stolen. He fell from his bike and the police tried to arrest him, only to be confronted by an angry crowd. Again, the situation escalated. Riots, it seemed, were contagious.

Because history is written by the winners, evidence of police harassment of people of colour in the early 1980s is hard to come by. But the Newham Monitoring Project bucked that trend. The organisation formed in 1980 after Asian teenager Akhtar Ali Baig was murdered by a gang of white skinheads on his way home from college. The following trial saw a judge comment that the murder was 'motivated by racial hatred'.[45] Frustrated by a lack of implementation of laws against racism, people in the community clubbed together to offer logistical support against racist harassment, and the Newham Monitoring Project was born. The grass-roots organisation campaigned against racist violence – including violence enacted by the police – until 2015, when it was forced to shut down due to lack of funds.

One part of the Newham Monitoring Project's work took place in the form of their annual reports, and their 1983 report gives a glimpse of what it was like to be black in east London at the time. During that year, the project received seventy-six reports of police harassment. Of those who were harassed by the police and subsequently arrested, forty-seven were released without charge. Those who *were* charged by the police were later released. Case studies in the report reveal a portrait of black families under siege. 'The home of Mr N and his family has been searched 4/5 times this year alone,' the report reads. 'Each time the police officers have had warrants with them, made out for stolen goods. Each time they have found no evidence and therefore have preferred no charges . . . the family expect their home to be invaded at any time. They live in constant fear of the next visit by the police.'[46]

There was also the case of forty-five-year-old Osei Owusu, who, after police turned up at his home asking to breathalyse him, refused. Minutes later, 'while he was in the bathroom in his house, 10–12 police officers smashed their way in, breaking down his front door. He was then dragged naked out of the bath, brutally assaulted with truncheons, and taken to Forest Gate Police Station. Once at the police station he was breathalysed. Three breathalyser tests on him failed.'

In one incident, police officers targeted a whole family. 'John Power was walking home after having been to a youth club,' the project recorded. 'As he was walking a police car drew up alongside him, by the pavement. The police officer in the car shouted, "Oi, come here you black bastard." John carried on walking. Then, fearing something may happen, [he] started to run home. The police officers followed him to his house, got to the front door, opened it and pulled John out and then proceeded to beat him.' When his father intervened, 'the police officers started beating him up as well.' When John's sister saw what was happening and screamed in fear, 'the police officer asked her to shut up and then pushed and hit her. All three were then put into different vehicles and taken to East Ham Police Station. They were then charged with obstruction and various charges of assaulting police officers.'

At the same time of this intense police brutality, there was also a movement towards restoring the eroded trust between people of colour and the police. Taking their lead from the United States, the police began to enact a new strategy. Community policing put officers in touch with people in local areas so that residents could get to know them. The late Chief Constable John Alderson strongly argued in the early 1980s that police should have more human involvement with the places they policed.[47] But this kind of community approach did not work to the benefit of black people. The Newham Monitoring Project's 1983 report highlighted this with a case in which an innocent black schoolboy was detained by the police. Eleven-year-old Shaun Robertson's secondary school had given a police officer who was investigating a robbery the names and addresses of every black child who attended the school. When the police officer mentioned that one of the suspects had two protruding front teeth, a school staff member let them know that Shaun had been to the orthodontist that same day. It was in this way that he became a suspect.

Camden's Committee for Community Relations described the double nature of the police in their 1984 Annual Report, writing 'Police strategy is two-faced. The brutality, the racism and the denial of civil liberties are meant, in the main, to be hidden from public view. The counter to this is "community policing", "neighbourhood watch", "the police/community consultative committee", "Community Liaison Officer" – all part of a public relations exercise to convince us that the police have a genuine interest in the community's well-being.'[48]

Oral histories from black people who lived through this time tend to maintain one common thread – that the police were not protecting them. The riots of 1981 saw a renewed interest in social cohesion from both local authorities and national government. An inquiry commissioned by the government was carried out by Lord Scarman to investigate the causes of the Brixton riots. The report was published by the end of that year. It recommended that the police put more effort into recruiting new officers from ethnic minority backgrounds. However, it concluded that institutional racism was not the problem – and instead pinpointed 'racial disadvantage' as an urgent social ill.

As a response to the report's recommendations, Hendon Police College set up its first Multicultural Unit. In 1982, John Fernandes was a black sociology lecturer at the now defunct Kilburn Polytechnic. Being an employee of Brent Council meant that John and some of his fellow lecturers were temporarily moved over to the local police college to teach. 'The Police College thought, oh my God, if [Lord Scarman's] coming here, we'd better start doing something to show we are dealing with this problem,' John told me over the phone from his home in the countryside.

Hendon Police College wanted John and his colleagues to develop a course about multiculturalism to teach to police cadets in training. Training to be a cadet was an internship-style scheme for young people that often led to full-time jobs in the police force. John was elected by his colleagues to head up Hendon Police College's multicultural unit. But he immediately ran into problems. The first red flag was that the college wanted to put an emphasis on multiculturalism rather than anti-racism. 'I was not very happy, as a black sociologist,' he explained. 'I wanted an anti-racist approach to it. Because the problem is not a black problem. It's not my culture, not my religion that is the problem. It is the racism of the white institutions.'

To go about proving that his anti-racist perspective would be more useful, he had to do a bit of research. 'If I was putting up a course as part of my submission on that course I had to provide evidence,' John said. 'I couldn't just make a statement and say I want to do an anti-racist course instead of a multicultural course.' He had to demonstrate that there was an already existing racist bias in the college's new recruits. 'As part of my research, I might have found that none of the cadets had a racist bias, maybe just a couple, so it's not a problem, so I'll do the multicultural course.'

His research saw him ask trainee police cadets at the college to write anonymous essays on the topic of 'blacks in Britain'. The responses were shocking.

'Blacks in Britain are a pest,' read one essay.[49] 'They come over here from some tin-pot banana country were [sic] they lived in huts and worked in the fields for cultivating rice and bananas, coconuts and tobacco, and take up residence in our already over-crowded island . . . They are, by nature unintelegent [sic] and can't at all be educated sufficiently to live in a civilised society of the Western world.'

'Housing conditions and facilities could be improved for them, but it is not worth it if they are going to abuse it,' read another essay.

'I think that all blacks are pains and should be ejected from society. On the whole most blacks are unem-ployed, like rastafarians [sic], who go round with big floppy hats, rollerskates and stereo radios smoking pot and sponging money off the state.'

'The black people in Britain claim that they are British w [sic] the help off [sic] words e.g., I've lived in Britain all my life and so [sic] my mum. This is just a load of junk in my mind because white peo-ple who live in, say Mozambique are not considered to be part of the country. Blacks are let of [sic] too much by this I mean a Police Officer arrest a black [person] may be called Racial Predjudist[sic]. If all the blacks were deported back to Africa or wherever [they] came from there would be less unemployment and therefore money for the Government to use for creating jobs.'

'When I saw them I thought, God almighty,' said John. 'That was why I had to make sure that it had to be an anti-racist course. So that I could explain to them, not to blame them for holding those views. You explain to them how it comes about that they all think the way they do.' Having acquired his evidence, he didn't take the essays straight to the Police College. Instead, he wrote up a syllabus for the course, and submitted it to Kilburn Polytechnic's academic board. When he got the permission he needed from the board, he took the syllabus to Hendon Police College. 'They were not willing to let me take the anti-racist stance,' he said. The college also asked him to hand over the racist essays that his course was based on. 'They were then arguing that I should give it to them because the students wrote them on the paper that was the property of the police.' John chose not to hand over the essays.

Faced with a predicament, he decided to stop teaching at the Police College. 'It was impossible to stay there,' he told me. 'How could I, as a black academic . . . I would be colluding if I stayed there and did the multicultural course. So I had to, whether my job was at stake or not. In all consciousness, since I'm black and I take an anti-racist approach, I had to leave. There was no way that I could stay there.'

Viewing the college's attitudes as indicative of a wider problem, he turned whistle-blower. The press had got wind of what was shaping up to be a scandal. *Eastern Eye*, a documentary TV series broadcast by London Weekend Television (now ITV London), aired a thirty-minute programme focused on what John had found. On the programme, a senior at the Police College responded to the scandal, saying, 'If I had the slightest suspicion that one of the young cadets had serious deep prejudices rather than shallowly expressed prejudices like that, then I would not recommend him to be a constable.'[50]

I asked John what happened to those trainee police cadets. 'There were no names, these [essays] were anonymous,' he said. 'Although I would know who they are, I would not give their names. It's professionalism.' It's impossible to know whether or not the essay writers went on to take jobs in the police force, or started careers in other professions. What we do know is that John Fernandes uncovered archaic attitudes that may have influenced policing at the time. His anti-racism course was sorely needed.

As would-be black politicians watched what was happening to communities they came from, they began to push for better black representation. Despite a very white leadership, back then the Labour Party had become the political home for the country's settled black and brown people. The party didn't have to work particularly hard for black support; it was about necessity, rather than a broad range of choice. Just twenty years earlier, the Conservative MP Peter Griffiths was elected to represent the Midlands constituency of Smethwick aided by the slogan 'if you want a nigger for a neighbour, vote Labour'.

Leo Dickson and Marc Wadsworth established the Labour Party's Black Sections in Vauxhall, south London, in 1983. It was a movement inside the party with the aim of championing black representation in the party (used in a political sense, black meant everyone who was not white). A general election took place in the same year, and a low turnout of black voters saw the Labour Party admit that they needed to do more to attract them. A pamphlet from the Vauxhall Labour Party published in 1984 reveals the thinking behind the formation of the sections, and the fiery debate the sections sparked among the Labour Party membership in the early days of setting up. In the pamphlet, Leo and Marc wrote: 'Our constituency covers an inner city area (Brixton) where manifestations of racism in Britain today are all pervasive.'[51] It wasn't surprising that the push for black representation in Britain's left-wing party came from south London – an area of the country that, at that point, was in its third decade of settled African and Caribbean migrants.

By the time Vauxhall Labour Party's pamphlet was published, a debate was raging in the national press about the legitimacy of the Labour Party's Black Sections. To gain ground in the party, as well as access to other black members, the section's organisers went to the party's executive committee to argue their case. In turn, the executive committee took it upon themselves to notify Labour Party members of all races of a meeting of a 'black caucus'. Leo and Marc were then put in the uncomfortable position of having to argue the case for black representation at some of the party's local branches. They were met with largely white opposition.

When the press got hold of party debates on the logistics of it all, it was reported as a race row. In correspondence to the Vauxhall branch in July 1984, the Labour Party's then leader Neil Kinnock expressed general support towards ending race discrimination in the party, but called the setting up of the Black Sections 'racially segregationist'.

The Labour Party Conference of 1984 was a significant one. The membership was voting on whether the Black Sections would be formally established in the party's constitution. Proposing the motion, the late Bernie Grant MP (then a councillor in the London borough of Haringey) said, 'Our problem is that blacks are not a priority in the Labour and trade union movement at the moment. Black Sections are here to ensure that they become a priority . . . we are concerned because we have been told that our leaders are against Black

Sections. One comrade has said that Black Sections will be turned into black ghettoes.'[52] Writing a report of the conference in *Race Today*, activist Darcus Howe spoke of an organised effort to crush the Black Sections: ' . . . The argument was a simple one,' he wrote. 'Black Sections divide the working class.'[53] The motion to formalise the Black Sections didn't pass, but their organising led to the election of Britain's first black Members of Parliament in 1987 – Diane Abbott, Paul Boateng and Bernie Grant.

Early one September morning in 1985, police officers broke down the front door of the Groce family in Brixton, south London. The house they burst into was home to thirty-seven-year-old Cherry Groce, and five of her six children. The family heard banging and shouting. Cherry left her eleven-year-old son Lee in her bedroom to find out what was going on. When she went to investigate, she was shot in the chest by a police officer. In a later statement, Cherry said that as she lay on the floor bleeding, police officers continued to shout at her, asking where her oldest son was.[54] Testimony from her son confirms this. Speaking to Channel 4 News in 2014, an older Lee recalled those early hours that changed his life. 'I just saw her on the floor. Lying on the floor. And I saw this policeman standing with the gun. He was basically pointing the gun towards her with his legs apart, and shouting, "Where's Michael Groce? Where's Michael Groce?" I was standing up on the bed and I was shouting, "What have you done to my mum?" The policeman turned the gun to me and said, "Shut up!"'[55] Michael Groce, twenty-one at the time, was suspected of being involved with an armed robbery. He didn't live with Cherry when the raid took place.

Cherry was moved to St Thomas' Hospital that same morning.[56] Meanwhile, local people got hold of the news of Cherry's shooting, and crowds began to gather on Brixton's streets. To disperse these crowds, police responded by cladding themselves in riot gear. Clashes between the community and the police led to two days of rioting.[57] There were burglaries and looting. Dozens of people sustained injuries, and a photojournalist trying to take pictures of the riot was killed.

In 1985, Tottenham's Broadwater Farm estate was heavily policed. But after what happened in Brixton, all police officers were ordered to leave.[58] On 5 October, nearly a week after the Brixton riots, Floyd Jarrett was stopped by the police while driving. His tax disc had expired. Because of a minor discrepancy between his car number plate and tax disc, he was arrested for suspected theft of the car. At Tottenham Police Station, off-duty officer Detective Sergeant

Randall suggested to his working colleagues that Floyd's house be searched for any other stolen goods. Keys to Floyd's mother's house were taken without his knowledge, and four officers let themselves in. One of those officers was DC Randall.

Inside they found Floyd's mother Cynthia, her daughter Patricia, and her small granddaughter. Later that year, Patricia would give evidence to an inquiry about her mother's death, in which she said, 'I saw Randall take his left arm and put it around my mother's shoulder and part of his body pushed her and she fell with her left arm out, breaking the small table.' DC Randall said that he didn't make contact with her. The inquiry, drawing on a coroner's report, decided that DC Randall's push was not deliberate, but that it had caused Cynthia Jarrett to fall. Either way, she collapsed. Cynthia was taken to North Middlesex Hospital, but died of a heart attack that evening. The same inquest that Patricia gave evidence to delivered a verdict of accidental death.

The following day, a crowd gathered outside Tottenham Police Station, calling for accountability for Cynthia's death. According to a report from community activist and organiser Stafford Scott,[59] DC Randall, the same officer who has since been proved to have been present for all pivotal points of the previous day, appeared at the window of the police station. Blaming Randall, protesters started to throw things at him. In the chaos that followed, over two hundred police officers were injured. A police officer, PC Blakelock, was killed by rioters.

A later inquiry into the events of that night commented: 'Let us recall what the evidence of the inquest and Magistrates Court revealed: – 1) That the officers who first stopped Floyd Jarrett made computer checks on his car, apparently for no other reason than he was a young black man. 2) That they arrested him and took him into custody on suspicion that his car was stolen which had little of any reasonable basis. 3) That they made a charge against him of assault which was found to be false.'[60] The officers' subsequent claim that the Jarrett family had shouted at them and had become abusive towards them while they were searching the house was also false.

In Brixton, Cherry Groce's gunshot wound left her paralysed from the waist down. Her children became her full-time carers. Twenty-six years later, aged sixty-three, she died of kidney failure. Her doctors confirmed that her death was directly linked to the gunshot wound. A 2014 inquest placed the responsibility of her death squarely on the police, finding that they failed to properly plan for the raid on the Groces' home, including adequately checking exactly who was living there.[61] That same year, Sir Bernard Hogan-Howe, head of the Metropolitan Police, apologised to the family.

Thirty years after the 1985 riots, and the cause of the abject neglect of black communities in Britain's big cities was laid bare for all to see. Files from 10 Downing Street released to the National Archives revealed that Oliver Letwin MP, then an adviser to Prime Minister Margaret Thatcher, chose not to accept proposals from cabinet ministers who were keen to implement positive action schemes in the inner cities and refurbish run-down and neglected estates. Letwin, still a Member of Parliament at the time of writing, refused these initiatives. 'Riots, criminality and social disintegration are caused solely by individual characters and attitudes,' he wrote to Thatcher alongside inner cities adviser Hartley Booth. 'So long as bad moral attitudes remain', they said, 'all efforts to improve the inner cities will founder. David Young's new entrepreneurs will set up in the disco and drug trade.'[62]

Combing through the literature on clashes between black people and the police, I noticed another clash – one of perspective. While some people called what happened in Tottenham and Brixton a riot, others called it an uprising – a rebellion of otherwise unheard people. I think there's truth in both perspectives, and that the extremity of a riot only ever reflects the extremity of the living conditions of said rioters. Language is important – and the term 'race riot' undoubtedly doubles down on ideas linking blackness and criminality, while overlooking what black people were reacting against. The conditions don't seem to have changed. When the London riots of August 2011 mirrored, almost step by step, what happened in Brixton in 1985, I wondered how often history would have to repeat itself before we choose to tackle the underlying problems.

I recall these histories not to obsessively comb over the past, but simply to know it. Perhaps I am betraying my ignorance, but until I went actively digging for black British histories, I didn't know them. I had heard that black people in Britain had always had a difficult relationship with the police. But I didn't ask why this was the case. It made more sense to me once I understood that innocent people had died, that homes were broken into with scant evidence for searching them, that teenagers and young adults were frisked in a ritual of humiliation. It makes sense to me now how animosity could brew in that environment, and why some insisted that the police were the biggest gang on the streets.

But I don't think my ignorance was an individual thing. That I had to go looking for significant moments in black British history suggests to me that I had been kept ignorant. While the black British story is starved of oxygen, the US struggle against racism is globalised into the story of the struggle against racism that we should look to for inspiration – eclipsing the black British story so much that we convince ourselves that Britain has never had a problem with race.

We need to stop lying to ourselves, and we need to stop lying to each other. To assume that there was no civil rights movement in the UK is not just untrue, it does a disservice to our black history, leaving gaping holes where the story of progress should be. Black Britain deserves a context. Speaking to the *Radio Times*, actor David Oyelowo highlighted the lack of historical British films about black people, saying, 'We make period dramas [in Britain], but there are almost never black people in them, even though we've been on these shores for hundreds of years. I remember taking a historical drama with a black figure at its centre to a British executive with greenlight power, and what they said was that if it's not Jane Austen or Dickens, the audience don't understand. And I thought, "OK – you are stopping people having a context for the country they live in and you are marginalising me. I can't live with that. So I've got to get out."[63] Faced with a collective forgetting, we must fight to remember.

I know that there is so much more history out there about people of colour in Britain, if you're willing to put in the effort to find it. After Britain voted to leave the European Union in June 2016, we were told reported hate crimes drastically grew in number, and that racism was on the rise in Britain again. But looking at our history shows racism does not erupt from nothing, rather it is embedded in British society. It's in the very core of how the state is set up. It's not external. It's in the system.

2

The System

On the evening of 22 April 1993, eighteen-year-old Stephen Lawrence left his uncle's house in Plumstead, south-east London, with his friend, Duwayne Brooks. As Stephen and Duwayne waited at a bus stop, Stephen started crossing the road to see if the bus was coming. He didn't make it to the other side. A later inquiry found that he was confronted by a gang of young white men around his age, who surrounded him as they approached. Stephen was set upon, and stabbed repeatedly. Duwayne fled, and Stephen followed, running over a hundred yards before collapsing due to sustained blood loss. He bled to death on the road.

A day after Stephen Lawrence's death, a letter listing the names of the people who turned out to be top suspects in the case was left in a telephone box near the bus stop. In the following months, that letter led to surveillance and arrests. Two people were charged. But by the end of July 1993, all the charges against them had been dropped, with the Metropolitan Police citing that evidence from Duwayne, the only witness to the crime, was not reliable enough. An inquest began later that year. It was halted after the barrister representing the family brought new evidence to the table. A year on, the Crown Prosecution Service chose not to prosecute any of the suspects, again saying that there was insufficient evidence to do so.

Stephen's parents launched a private prosecution against three of the suspects. Meanwhile, police surveillance saw the same men suspected of murdering Stephen Lawrence using violent and racist language. By April 1996, the private prosecution launched by his family had failed. This time the judge ruled that evidence from Stephen's friend Duwayne Brooks, was not valid.

In 1997, the decision from the inquest initiated in 1993 was announced. Although each of the five suspects refused to answer the questions put to them, a verdict of an unlawful killing in an 'unprovoked racist attack' was delivered. Later that year, Kent Police investigated police conduct after an official complaint from Stephen Lawrence's parents to the Police Complaints Authority. The result nine months later would find 'significant weaknesses, omissions and lost opportunities' in the way that the police dealt with the investigation of Stephen Lawrence's death. Kent Police's Deputy Chief Constable Bob Ayling spoke to the BBC's *Newsnight* programme two years later, calling the police's investigation into Stephen's death 'seriously flawed'. Another key witness had come forward, Ayling revealed, but he had been seen by a low-ranking police officer, and his testimony had been dismissed. Three phone calls had been made to the police by a woman who sounded like she was close to one of the suspects, but her statements were not adequately followed up.

Now, it is public knowledge that the process of convicting Stephen's killers was tantamount to a charade. But back in 1997, the public still had faith that the police could solve this crime. In July of that year, the then Home Secretary Jack Straw announced that there would be a judicial inquiry into Stephen Lawrence's death and the following police investigation. It was to be chaired by a High Court judge named Sir William Macpherson.

Dissatisfied with the police's handling of the case and their seemingly unending search for justice, in 1998 Stephen Lawrence's family called on then Metropolitan Police Commissioner Sir Paul Condon to resign. He responded not by resigning, but with an apology. 'I deeply regret that we have not brought Stephen's racist murderers to justice and I would like to personally apologise again today to Mr and Mrs Lawrence for our failure,' he told the inquiry while giving evidence. 'We have heard what people have been saying and I accept that a central concern is that the Met is racist. I acknowledge that we have not done enough to combat racist crime and harassment.'

Despite this admission, Sir Paul chose not to yield to any suggestions that the Metropolitan Police were *institutionally* racist. Speaking to the press at the time, Doreen, Stephen's mother and the figurehead of the Lawrence family's campaign for justice, said, 'Sir Paul has got fine words. I still have not been given the answer as to why Stephen's killers are still free.'[1]

In a later statement, the Lawrences said: 'Maybe we need another public inquiry into police corruption for the Commissioner to then accept that these boys were protected in some way. If it hadn't been for this inquiry, the Commissioner would still be saying that officers did everything they could to bring our son's killer to justice.'[2]

The report of Sir William Macpherson's public inquiry was published in February 1999. It concluded that the investigation into the death of Stephen Lawrence 'was marred by a combination of profession-al incompetence, institutional racism and a failure of leadership by senior officers'. This institutional racism, the report explained, is 'the collective failure of an organisation to provide an appropriate and professional service to people because of their colour, culture, or ethnic origin. It can be seen or detected in processes, attitudes and behaviour which amount to discrimination through unwitting prejudice, ignorance, thoughtlessness and racist stereotyping which disadvantage minority ethnic people.'[3] Most importantly, the report described institutional racism as a form of collective behaviour, a workplace culture supported by a structural status quo, and a consensus – often excused and ignored by authorities. Amongst its many recommendations, the report suggested that the police force boost its black representation, and that all officers be trained in racism awareness and cultural diversity.

In 2004, and after another review, the Crown Prosecution Service announced that there wasn't enough evidence to prosecute any of those suspected of murdering Stephen Lawrence. In 2005, a change in the law saw an 800-year-old ban on double jeopardy lifted, meaning that it was no longer illegal to try suspects twice for the same crime. A review of forensic evidence led to a new trial of those suspected of murdering Stephen Lawrence.

On 4 January 2012, *nineteen years* after Stephen's death, two out of the five suspected men were finally found guilty and sentenced for his murder. When Gary Dobson and David Norris killed Stephen, they were teenagers. By the time Dobson and Norris were jailed, they were adult men, in their mid- to late-thirties. While Stephen Lawrence's life was frozen at eighteen, theirs had continued, unhindered, in part aided by the police.

Both men received life sentences. When passing the sentence, Judge Mr Justice Treacy described the crime as a 'murder which scarred the conscience of the nation'. It was a monumental day for Britain, if long overdue. Many were wondering how the police had failed so catastrophically, and why justice took so long.

I was three years old when Stephen Lawrence died, and I was twenty-two when two of his killers were convicted and jailed. Doreen Lawrence's struggle for justice stretched out alongside the timeline of my childhood. Reports of the Stephen Lawrence case were some of the only TV news I remember absorbing as a child. A vicious racist attack, a black boy stabbed and bleeding to death, a mother desperate for justice. His death haunted me. I began to lose faith in the system.

I used to have a feeling, a vague sense of security in the back of my mind, that if I returned home one day to find my belongings ransacked and my valuables gone, I could call the police and they would help me. But if the case of Stephen Lawrence taught me anything, it was that there are occasions when the police cannot be trusted to act fairly.

For so long, the bar of racism has been set by the easily condemnable activity of white extremists and white nationalism. The white extremists are always roundly condemned by the big three political parties.

The reactionary white pride sentiment, so often positioned in opposition to social progress, has never really gone away. It manifests in the ebb and flow of groups like the National Front, the British National Party and the English Defence League. Their political activity, whether it is storming down busy city streets in hoodies and balaclavas, or suited up and feigning respectability at their political conferences, has real-life consequences for people who aren't white and British.

If all racism was as easy to spot, grasp and denounce as white extremism is, the task of the anti-racist would be simple. People feel that if a racist attack has not occurred, or the word 'nigger' has not been uttered, an action can't be racist. If a black person hasn't been spat at in the street, or a suited white extremist politician hasn't lamented the lack of British jobs for British workers, it's not racist (and if the suited politician *has* said that, then the racism of his statement will be up for debate, because it's not racist to want to protect your country!). Then there's the glaringly obvious point – if white extremism really *is* the bar at which we set all racism, why and how does racism thrive in quarters in which those in charge do not align themselves with white extremist politics? The problem must run deeper.

We tell ourselves that good people can't be racist. We seem to think that true racism only exists in the hearts of evil people. We tell ourselves that racism is about moral values, when instead it is about the survival strategy of systemic power. When swathes of the population vote for politicians and political efforts that explicitly use racism as a campaigning tool, we tell ourselves that huge sections of the electorate simply *cannot be racist*, as that would render them heartless monsters. But this isn't about good and bad people.

The covert nature of structural racism is difficult to hold to account. It slips out of your hands easily, like a water-snake toy. You can't spot it as easily as a St George's flag and a bare belly at an English Defence League march. It's much more respectable than that.

I appreciate that the word structural can feel and sound abstract. *Structural*. What does that even mean? I choose to use the word structural rather than institutional because I think it is built into spaces much broader than our more traditional institutions. Thinking of the big picture helps you see the structures. Structural racism is dozens, or hundreds, or thousands of people with the same biases joining together to make up one organisation, and acting accordingly. Structural racism is an impenetrably white workplace culture set by those people, where anyone who falls outside of the culture must conform or face failure. *Structural* is often the only way to capture what goes unnoticed – the silently raised eyebrows, the implicit biases, snap judgements made on perceptions of competency. In the same year that I decided to no longer talk to white people about race, the British Social Attitudes survey saw a significant increase in the number of people who were happy to admit to their own racism.[4] The sharpest rise in those self-admitting were, according to a *Guardian* report, 'white, professional men between the ages of 35 and 64, highly educated and earning a lot of money'.[5] This is what structural racism looks like. It is not just about personal prejudice, but the collective effects of bias. It is the kind of racism that has the power to drastically impact people's life chances. Highly educated, high-earning white men are very likely to be landlords, bosses, CEOs, head teachers, or university vice chancellors. They are almost certainly people in positions that influence others' lives. They are almost certainly the kind of people who set workplace cultures. They are unlikely to boast about their politics with colleagues or acquaintances because of the social stigma of being associated with racist views. But their racism is covert. It doesn't manifest itself in spitting at strangers in the street. Instead, it lies in an apologetic smile while explaining to an unlucky soul that they didn't get the job. It manifests itself in the flick of a wrist that tosses a CV in the bin because the applicant has a foreign-sounding name.

The national picture is grim. Research from a number of different sources shows how racism is weaved into the fabric of our world. This demands a collective redefinition of what it means to be racist, how racism manifests, and what we must do to end it.

It seems like black people face a disadvantage at every significant step in their lives. Let's say that a black boy starts his first day at school, the first British institution he will pass through independent of his parents. Mum and Dad are full of hope for what he might become – an artist, a doctor, the next prime minister – and this is where he will set himself up to achieve those wished-for goals. But perhaps his parents should temper their excitement, because evidence suggests that the odds will be stacked against him. According to the Department for Education, a black schoolboy in England is around three times more likely to be permanently excluded compared to the whole school population.[6] But let's say that our black boy (and it's always a boy – there's little to no research in this area focused on the life chances of black girls) avoids being excluded and makes it far enough into his school journey to take exams. He won't be explicitly aware of the invisible barriers placed in his way, but they will exist. At the age of eleven, when he is preparing to take his SATs, research indicates that he will be systematically marked down by his own teachers – a phenomenon that is remedied when examiners who don't teach at his school mark his exam papers.[7] It will take anonymity to get him the grade he deserves.

In the spirit of optimism, let us insist that our imaginary black child gets into a good secondary school, studies a subject he loves, and becomes determined to go to university. The evidence suggests his fortunes might drastically change as a greater proportion of black students than white students progress to higher education after sixth form or college. But, along race lines, access to Britain's prestigious universities is unequal, with black students less likely to be accepted into a high-ranking, research-intensive Russell Group university than their white counterparts.[8]

Perhaps the black child – now blossoming into an adult – has got the grades he needed, and is accepted into a good university, despite the odds being stacked against him. Three years later, and he's furiously refreshing his university's results page, eagerly awaiting the degree classification that will be his ticket to graduate employment. He's hoping for a 2:1 at least, but has his fingers crossed for a 1st – because all the job ads he's browsed so far explicitly mention that graduates with a 2:2 degree or lower shouldn't waste their time applying.

Although we don't want to pour a bucket of water over his dreams, it's not looking good. Between 2012 and 2013, the highest proportion of UK students to receive the lowest-degree ranking – a third or a pass – was among black students, with the lowest proportion being white students.[9] Given that black kids are more likely than white kids to move into higher education, it's spurious to suggest that this attainment gap is down to a lack of intelligence, talent, or aspiration. It's worth looking at the distinct lack of black and brown faces teaching at university to see what might contribute to this systematic failure. In 2016, it was revealed by the Higher Education Statistics Agency that almost 70 per cent of the professors teaching in British universities are white men.[10] It's a dire indication of what universities think intelligence looks like.

Because he exists in this book only to make a point, we can imagine that the young black man makes it out of education in one piece, with a good degree from a good university, and his eyes fixed upon getting a good job, like all determined graduates. Although he won't know it, outside of education, the drastic racial disparities continue. He might look at the white kids he went to university with and watch them effortlessly transition from student booze-culture-loving lager louts to slick-young-professional status. Full of hope, our black boy will still continue to send out CVs, because he believes in meritocracy. There's no difference between him and his white peers, he thinks. They sat in the same lectures and read the same books. But his potential employers might not see it that way. In 2009, researchers working on behalf of the Department of Work and Pensions sent job applications with similar education, skills and work history to a number of prospective employers. The only distinctive difference in the applications were names – they either sounded white British, or they didn't. The researchers found that the applicants with white-sounding names were called to interview far more often than those with African- or Asian-sounding names.[11] 'High levels of name-based net discrimination were found in favour of white applicants,' the report commented.

So, our young black man could find himself unemployed and scraping by for a very long time. Research in 2012 found that austerity was hitting young black men particularly hard, with their demographic facing a sharp rise in unemployment, predating even the 2008 recession. A staggering 45 per cent of black sixteen- to twenty-four-year-olds were out of work in 2012 compared with just 27 per cent in 2002.[12] More broadly, ethnic minority people in England and Wales have historically dealt with lower rates of employment and higher rates of unemployment than white people.[13] Looking at twenty years of census data between 1991 and 2011, you'll see that black men have had consistently high rates of unemployment – more than double those of their white counterparts. The same disadvantage is echoed in black Caribbean women and black African women compared to white women.

There is more to life than getting a good education and a decent job, though. Productivity alone does not make a worthwhile human being. What about our young black man's social and personal life? On his way to meet friends, or to school or work, he might find himself stopped and searched by the police. In fact, he will almost certainly have some contact with the police. A 2013 British report revealed that black people are twice as likely to be charged with drugs possession, despite lower rates of drug use. Black people are also more likely to receive a harsher police response (being five times more likely to be charged rather than cautioned or warned) for possession of drugs.[14] That probably won't come as a surprise to him, though, and he will be used to the feeling of an overbearing police presence in his life. He will have almost certainly seen his brothers, uncles and older male friends routinely patted down by the police. In fact, relentless policing of the black community in Britain means that black people are over-represented on the National Criminal Intelligence DNA Database. Although there's no recent official figures, a 2009 report from the Equalities and Human Rights Commission estimated that roughly 30 per cent of all black men living in Britain are on the National DNA Database, compared with about 10 per cent of white men and 10 per cent of Asian men. They also estimated that black men are about four times more likely than white men to have their DNA profiles stored on the police database. This led the commission to comment '. . . we are concerned that the high proportion of black men recorded on the database (estimated to be at least one in three black men) is creating an impression that a single race group represents an "alien wedge" of criminality.'[15]

We must hope that, later on in his life, our black man is not adversely affected by health problems, either physical or mental. A 2003 NHS England report confirmed that 'there is a uniformity of findings that people of African and African Caribbean backgrounds are more at risk than any other ethnic group in England to be admitted to psychiatric hospitals under the compulsory powers of the Mental Health Act' – that's being sectioned against your will.[16] In the same year, an inquiry into the death of David Bennett, a black man who died in a psychiatric unit, added '[black people] tend to receive higher doses of anti-psychotic medication than white people with similar health problems. They are generally regarded by mental health staff as more aggressive, more alarming, more dangerous and more difficult to treat. Instead of being discharged back into the community they are more likely to remain as long-term in-patients.'[17] As our imaginary black man gets older, he is less likely to receive a diagnosis of dementia than his white counterparts. If he does, he will receive it at a later stage than a white British person.[18]

Our black man's life chances are hindered and warped at every stage. There isn't anything notably, individually racist about the people who work in all of the institutions he interacts with. Some of these people will be black themselves. But it doesn't really matter what race they are. They are both in and of a society that is structurally racist, and so it isn't surprising when these unconscious biases seep out into the work they do when they interact with the general public. With a bias this entrenched, in too many levels of society, our black man can try his hardest, but he is essentially playing a rigged game. He may be told by his parents and peers that if he works hard enough, he can overcome anything. But the evidence shows that that is not true, and that those who do are exceptional to be succeeding in an environment that is set up for them to fail. Some will even tell them that if they are successful enough to get on the radar of an affirmative action scheme, then it's because of tokenism rather than talent.

The statistics are devastating. But they are not the result of a lack of black excellence, talent, education, hard work or creativity. There are other, more sinister forces at play here.

There are swathes of evidence to suggest that your life chances are obstructed and slowed down if you are born black in Britain. Despite this, many insist that any attempt to level the playing ground is special treatment, and that we must focus on equality of opportunity, without realising that levelling the playing ground *is* enabling equality of opportunity. This is far from new. Over a decade ago, Neil Davenport wrote in *Spiked Online* that 'affirmative action enforces rather than overcomes notions of equal racial abilities'.[19] Instead of being seen as a solution to a systemic problem, positive discrimination is frequently pinpointed as one of the key accelerators in rampant 'political correctness', and quotas are some of the most hotly contested methods of eliminating homogeneous workplaces in recent years. The method works a little bit like this: senior people in an organisation realise their workplace doesn't reflect the reality of the world they live in (either because of internal or external pressure), so they implement recruitment tactics to redress the balance. Quotas have been suggested as a strategy in many sectors – from politics, to sport, to theatre – and they always receive a backlash.

In 2002, America's National Football League introduced measures to address the lack of black managers in the sport. Named after the NFL's diversity committee chair Dan Rooney, the Rooney rule worked through a rather mild method of opening up opportunities for people of colour. When a senior coaching or operations position became available, teams were required to interview at least one black or minority ethnic person for the job. This was a shortlist requirement only.

Teams were under no obligation to hire said person. The rule wasn't a quota. Neither was it an all-black shortlist, or a rigid percentage target. Instead, it was an incredibly tame 'softly softly' attempt to rebalance the scales. The Rooney rule was implemented a year after it was introduced. A decade after the rule's implementation, the evidence was showing that it was working. In those ten years, twelve new black coaches had been hired across the States, and seventeen teams had been led by either a black or Latino coach, some even in quick succession. The general consensus was that the sport's bosses had begun to see candidates that they wouldn't have previously considered.

Around the time of the rule's tenth birthday, its success in the US led to the idea being floated in British football. For some football bosses, it was considered a good way to quell the sport's ugly history of overt racism, a way to heal the jagged wounds of monkey noises and bananas thrown at black players on the pitch in years past. Then Football Association chairman Greg Dyke gave the idea a nod, confirming to the BBC in 2014 that the FA's inclusion advisory board were considering some version of the rule. In British football, as of 2015, the numbers on race were pitiful. Despite overall black and ethnic minority representation of 25 per cent in both leagues, there was only one black manager in the Premier League, and just six black managers in the Football League. There were no black managers

in Scotland's top four divisions, and just one black manager in Wales' Elite League.[20]

Despite its utterly inoffensive nature, the idea of
implementing the Rooney rule in British football sent
the nation into a spin. Chairman of Blackpool FC Karl
Oyston called it 'tokenism' and 'an absolute insult' to
people in the sport.[21] Carlisle United manager Keith
Curle essentially called it a box-ticking exercise.[22]
Richard Scudamore, chief executive of the Premier
League, introduced plans to develop a pool of black
coaches instead, and called the Rooney rule unnecessary.[23] The way it was spoken about, you'd think that
the FA's plans weren't suggesting having one person of
colour on an interview shortlist, but instead were asking team heads to walk into their local supermarket
and offer their most high-level jobs to the first random
black person they saw in the vegetable aisle. In 2016,
the English Football League opted to put forward proposals to implement the Rooney rule on a mandatory
basis. The Premier League chose not to entertain the
idea even on a voluntary basis.[24]

Around the same time as Britain's Rooney rule
conversation, a similar debate was taking place in the
business sector. Then Business Secretary Vince Cable
tabled plans to diversify business boards, announcing
an aim of 20 per cent black and ethnic minority
FTSE100 directors in just five years. Research in the
same year found that over half of FTSE100 companies

didn't have a single person of colour at board level.[25] With the conversation about boardrooms previously focusing solely on a very white version of gender, Cable's intervention was refreshing. But, again, there was pushback against the idea, with the director general of the Institute of Directors, Simon Walker, telling the *Telegraph*: 'Businesses seek to appoint board members on the basis of competence. They may not always make good decisions but there is little sign of systematic racial prejudice at the top of British business.'[26]

In 2015, a debate pondering the possibility of quotas to secure an increased number of women and people of colour judges prompted senior judge Lord Justice Leveson to announce to a lecture hall that the idea was entirely demeaning. 'Creating a principle of appointment not because of merit but in order to achieve gender or ethnic balance', he told his audience, 'will inevitably lead to the inference that those appointments are most decidedly not based on merit alone.'[27] Although it was established in 1875, the High Court only welcomed its first black judge, Dame Linda Dobbs, in 2004. She was born in Sierra Leone, received her legal education in Britain, and was called to the bar in 1981. In an interview with video archive *First 100 Years*, she detailed some of the discrimination she faced, saying, 'It was difficult to complain about things in those days. There were no procedures. None of that was recorded, so to try and prove that, you know, you were discriminated against was very difficult indeed.'[28] Dame Linda Dobbs retired from the High Court in 2013. In 2015, just 7 per cent of judges across courts and tribunals were black or from an ethnic minority background.

When it comes to women, lack of representation prompts calls for all-out quotas. A 2015 London School of Economics report called for gender quotas in all senior public and private positions. When a survey in the same year showed that less than 20 per cent of senior managers in the City of London were female, women in the financial sector began calling for quotas to tackle the over-representation of men.[29] And when surveyed in 2013 over half the women working in construction – many of whom were working in companies where women were just 10 per cent of the workforce – supported the idea of quotas.[30]

But when it comes to race, the language used to raise awareness of similar issues is much less definitive. Instead of talk of quotas – where progress can be measured with numbers – the solutions posed are vague. The head of the Office for Standards in Education, Children's Services and Skills suggested positive discrimination in teaching recruitment in 2015, stressing that the ethnic mix of teachers should reflect the pupils they teach.[31] When he was head of the Greater Manchester Police, Sir Peter Fahy called for a change in equality legislation so that police constabularies could use positive discrimination when hiring black police officers, but he was sure to let it be known that it wasn't about 'targets'.[32] It seems that the root of the problem of both the under-representation of race and gender is essentially the same, but the solutions proposed for each are radically different. When there are no hard targets behind programmes of positive discrimination, initiatives are in danger of looking like they're doing something without actually achieving much.

Positive discrimination initiatives are often vehemently opposed. Descriptions of the work addressing the over-representation of whiteness inevitably reduce it to tokenism, nothing more than an insult to the good hard-working people who get their high-ranking jobs on merit alone. Whenever I do the panel-event circuit, meritocracy and quotas tend to be an issue that rests heavily on audiences' minds. The main questions asked are: is it fair? Do quotas mean that women and people of colour are receiving special treatment, getting leg-ups others can't access? Surely we should be judging candidates on merit alone? The underlying assumption to all opposition to positive discrimination is that it just isn't fair play.

The insistence is on merit, insinuating that any current majority white leadership in any industry has got there through hard work and no outside help, as if whiteness isn't its own leg-up, as if it doesn't imply a familiarity that warms an interviewer to a candidate. When each of the sectors I mentioned earlier have such dire racial representation, you'd have to be fooling yourself if you really think that the homogeneous glut of middle-aged white men currently clogging the upper echelons of most professions got there purely through talent alone. We don't live in a meritocracy, and to pretend that simple hard work will elevate all to success is an exercise in wilful ignorance.

Opposing positive discrimination based on apprehensions about getting the best person for the job means inadvertently revealing what you think talent looks like, and the kind of person in which you think talent resides. Because, if the current system worked correctly, and if hiring practices were successfully recruiting and promoting the right people for the right jobs in all circumstances, I seriously doubt that so many leadership positions would be occupied by white middle-aged men. Those who insist on fairness fail to recognise that the current state of play is far from fair. When pressed on lack of representation, some like to cite the racial demographics in Britain, saying that because the minority of the population isn't white, that percentage and that percentage only should be represented in organisations. This mathematical approach is the true tokenism. It is an obsession with bodies in the room rather than recruiting the right people who will work in the interests of the marginalised. Representation doesn't always mean that the represinter will work in the favour of those who need representation.

In the interests of honesty, I must disclose that there was a time when I thought efforts to increase black representation were suspicious. I didn't understand why there was a need for it. I could never understand why, growing up, my mum had also instructed me to work twice as hard as my white counterparts. As far as I was concerned, we were all the same. So when she forwarded me an application form for a diversity scheme at a national newspaper when I was at university, I felt angry, indignant, and ashamed. At first I resisted applying for it at all, telling her, 'If I'm going to compete against my white peers, I'm doing it on a level playing ground.' After some cajoling on her part, I applied, got through to the interview stage, and eventually landed the internship.

A few things were apparent to me from the outset when working there. At the interview stage, I was one of the few applicants who weren't currently studying at, or a graduate of, Oxbridge. Then, during the internship itself, I quickly understood why it was needed in the first place. To me at the time, internship schemes looking for specifically black and minority ethnic participants seemed fundamentally unfair, but once I got through the door, the black faces working there were more likely to be doing the catering or cleaning than setting the news agenda. Moreover, back then, it was rare for internships to be formalised at all. Until fairly recently, media internships had been running on word of mouth and nepotism, relying on someone who knew someone who knew someone. If you didn't have someone in your family, friendship group or extended network who was in the profession, or you weren't prepared to work for free, you were cut out. I worked on a shop floor for months so I could afford to work unpaid for three weeks, and my family lived in London, so my living expenses were minimal.

It was in that moment that I had to reluctantly accept that pushes for positive discrimination were not about turning the whole place black at the expense of white people, but instead were simply about reflecting the society an organisation serves.

Structural racism is never a case of innocent and pure, persecuted people of colour versus white people intent on evil and malice. Rather, it is about how Britain's relationship with race infects and distorts equal opportunity. I think that we placate ourselves with the fallacy of meritocracy by insisting that we just don't *see* race. This makes us feel progressive. But this claim to not see race is tantamount to compulsory assimilation. My blackness has been politicised against my will, but I don't want it wilfully ignored in an effort to instil some sort of precarious, false harmony. And, though many placate themselves with the colour-blindness lie, the aforementioned drastic differences in life chances along race lines show that while it might be being preached by our institutions, it's not being practised.

When we live in the age of colour-blindness, and fool ourselves with the lie of meritocracy, some will have to be silent in order for others to thrive. In 2014 I interviewed black feminist academic Dr Kimberlé Crenshaw, she elaborated on the politics of colour-blindness. 'It's this idea that to eliminate race, you have to eliminate all discourse, including efforts to acknowledge racial structures and hierarchies and address them,' she said. 'It's those cosmopolitan-thinking, twenty-first-century, "not trying to carry the burdens of the past and you shouldn't either" [people]. Along with them are people who consider themselves left, progressive and very critical, who in some ways join up with the post-racial liberals and colour-blind conservatives to say, "if we really want to get beyond race, we have to stop talking race".'

Colour-blindness is a childish, stunted analysis of racism. It starts and ends at 'discriminating against a person because of the colour of their skin is bad', without any accounting for the ways in which structural power manifests in these exchanges. With an analysis so immature, this definition of racism is often used to silence people of colour attempting to articulate the racism we face. When people of colour point this out, they're accused of being racist against white people, and the accountability avoidance continues. Colour-blindness does not accept the legitimacy of structural racism or a history of white racial dominance.

Repeatedly telling ourselves – and worse still, telling our children – that we are all equal is a misdirected yet well-intentioned lie. We can just about recognise the overt racial segregation of old. But indulging in the myth that we are all equal denies the economic, polit-ical and social legacy of a British society that has his-torically been organised by race. The reality is that, in material terms, we are nowhere near equal. This state of play is violently unjust. It's a social construct that was created to continue racial dominance and injus-tice. And the *difference* people of colour are vaguely aware of since birth is not benign. It is fraught with racism, racist stereotyping, and for women, racialised misogyny.

White children are taught not to 'see' race, whereas children of colour are taught – often with no explana-tion – that we must work twice as hard as our white counterparts if we wish to succeed. There is a disparity here. Colour-blindness does not get to the root of rac-ism. Meanwhile, it is nigh-on impossible for children of colour to educate ourselves out of racist stereotyping, though if we accumulate enough individual wealth, we can pretend that we are no longer affected by it.

Not seeing race does little to deconstruct racist structures or materially improve the conditions which people of colour are subject to daily. In order to dismantle unjust, racist structures, we must see race. We must see who benefits from their race, who is disproportionately impacted by negative stereotypes about their race, and to who power and privilege is bestowed upon – earned or not – because of their race, their class, and their gender. Seeing race is essential to changing the system.

3

WHAT IS WHITE PRIVILEGE?

When I was four, I asked my mum when I would turn white, because all the good people on TV were white, and all the villains were black and brown. I considered myself to be a good person, so I thought that I would turn white eventually. My mum still remembers the crestfallen look on my face when she told me the bad news.

Neutral is white. The default is white. Because we are born into an already written script that tells us what to expect from strangers due to their skin colour, accents and social status, the whole of humanity is coded as white. Blackness, however, is considered the 'other' and therefore to be suspected. Those who are coded as a threat in our collective representation of humanity are not white. These messages were so powerful that four-year-old me had already recognised them, watching television, noticing that all the characters who looked like me were criminals at worst, and sassy sidekicks at best.

How can I define white privilege? It's so difficult to describe an absence. And white privilege is an absence of the negative consequences of racism. An absence of structural discrimination, an absence of your race being viewed as a problem first and foremost, an absence of 'less likely to succeed because of my race'. It is an absence of funny looks directed at you because you're believed to be in the wrong place, an absence of cultural expectations, an absence of violence enacted on your ancestors because of the colour of their skin, an absence of a lifetime of subtle marginalisation and othering – exclusion from the narrative of being human. Describing and defining this absence means to some extent upsetting the centring of whiteness, and reminding white people that their experience is not the norm for the rest of us. It is, of course, much easier to identify when you don't have it, and I watch as an outsider to the insularity of whiteness. I coveted whiteness once, but I knew in the back of my mind that conning myself into assimilation would only ever make me a poor imitation of what I would never be.

You might be surprised to learn that it was a white man who first gave white privilege a name. Theodore W. Allen was born in Indianapolis, Indiana in 1919. In his adulthood he was active in the trade union movement. Deeply affected by the American civil rights movement in the 1960s, his reading of black writers like W. E. B. Du Bois led him to start exploring what he called 'white-skin privilege'. His was an anti-capitalist perspective on race in the labour movement. In 1967, riffing on the civil rights movement's much-used phrase 'an injury to one is an injury to all', he wrote '. . . the injury dealt out to the black worker has its counterpart in the privilege of the white worker. To expect the white worker to help wipe out the injury to the Negro is to ask him to oppose his own interests.'[1]

To some, the word 'privilege' in the context of whiteness invokes images of a life lived in the lap of luxury, enjoying the spoils of the super-rich. When I talk about white privilege, I don't mean that white people have it easy, that they've never struggled, or that they've never lived in poverty. But white privilege is the fact that if you're white, your race will almost certainly positively impact your life's trajectory in some way. And you probably won't even notice it.

White privilege is one of the reasons why I stopped talking to white people about race. Trying to convince stony faces of disbelief has never appealed to me. The idea of white privilege forces white people who aren't actively racist to confront their own complicity in its continuing existence. White privilege is dull, grinding complacency. It is par for the course in a world in which drastic race inequality is responded to with a shoulder shrug, considered just the norm.

We could all do with examining how the system unfairly benefits us personally. A few years back, confronted with a four-hour round trip of a commute, I found that the only way to keep costs down and still make it to work was to get the train halfway, and cycle for the rest of the journey. An uncomfortable truth dawned on me as I lugged my bike up and down flights of stairs in commuter-town train stations: the majority of public transport I'd been travelling on was not easily accessible. No ramps, no lifts. Nigh-on impossible to access for parents with buggies, or people using wheelchairs, or people with mobility issues, like a frame or a cane. Before I'd had my own wheels to carry, I'd never noticed this problem. I'd been oblivious to the fact that this lack of accessibility was affecting hundreds of people. And it was only when the issue became close to me that I began to feel infuriated by it.

I have to be honest with myself. When I write as an outsider, I am also an insider in so many ways. I am university-educated, able-bodied, and I speak and write in ways very similar to those I criticise. I walk and talk like them, and part of that is why I am taken seriously. As I write about shattering perspectives and disrupting faux objectivity, I have to remember that there are factors in my life that bolster my voice above others.

Racism is often confused with prejudice, and is sometimes used interchangeably. It's another retort wielded against anti-racists, who have to listen to those who wish to undermine the movement muster up outrage about discrimination against white people because they are white. Some black people hold a burning hatred for white people, they will say, and it's unacceptable. It's 'reverse racism', they insist. Prejudice is real across communities of colour. Years ago, buying myself a lunch of Caribbean food, I was greeted by a smiling owner behind the counter who waited until his white customers had left before confiding in me that he saves the best cuts of meat for 'people like us'. Yes, that man was prejudiced. Yes, my lunch was delicious. No, the owner of the cafe couldn't possibly affect the life chances of his white customers with his feelings against them. All he could affect in any terms was their lunch.

This is the difference between racism and prejudice. There is an unattributed definition of racism that defines it as prejudice plus power. Those disadvantaged by racism can certainly be cruel, vindictive and prejudiced. Everyone has the capacity to be nasty to other people, to judge them before they get to know them. But there simply aren't enough black people in positions of power to enact racism against white people on the kind of grand scale it currently operates at against black people. Are black people over-represented in the places and spaces where prejudice could really take effect? The answer is almost always no.

A few years ago I got into a conversation with a friend's white, French girlfriend about racism. I spoke to her honestly about my experiences. It was going well, and she was telling me about the troubles she faced as the youngest and only woman in her work-place, often having to work twice as hard to prove herself as competent to her employers. We were get-ting along, and we found we had common ground. I told her about an experience of being passed over for a job I'd interviewed for and finding out through mutual friends that the position had gone to a white woman my age with almost identical experience to me. I had felt the slap in the face of structural racism, the kind of thing you only hear about in statistics about black unemployment, but never hear about from the people affected by it.

Then she said, 'You don't know if that was racism. How do you know it wasn't something else?' She told me about her anger and fear after being accused of rac-ism by an Algerian man. She said how angry it made her feel, that people can use accusations of racism to stop white people talking, that maybe the man should have considered that people didn't like him because he didn't behave very well. She said she had felt intimi-dated because he was a man, she said she thought he might get aggressive.

I was naive. We had resonated beforehand, so I had good faith in her humanity, I thought she might be able to accept the structural conditions that allowed a situation like this one to happen. So I tried to encourage her to consider the suspicion and anger of a person who has suffered racism their entire lives. I thought I might be able to persuade her to think outside of herself and question the wider context, but then every sentence she said sounded like every word I've ever heard from people defending whiteness. It's like they all learn the lines from the same sheet.

Then I considered the social implications of the logical outcome of our exchange, where the consensus would be that I am wrong, because that's how the white status quo maintains itself. If I'd argued with her, I would put myself at risk of no longer being welcome in that particular houseshare, because I would have 'created an atmosphere'. I would be considered a 'reverse racist', an angry, unreasonable troublemaker, maybe even a violence sympathiser. This kind of social exclusion did not seem worth it. So I said nothing.

White privilege manifests itself in everyone and no one. Everyone is complicit, but no one wants to take on responsibility. Challenging it can have real social implications. Because it's a many-headed hydra, you have to be careful about the white people you trust when it comes to discussing race and racism. You don't have the privilege of approaching conversations about racism with the assumption that the other participants will be on the same plane as you. Raising racism in a conversation is like flicking a switch. It doesn't matter if it's a person you've just met, or a person you've always felt safe and comfortable with. You're never sure when a conversation about race and racism will turn into one where you were scared for your physical safety or social position.

White privilege is a manipulative, suffocating blanket of power that envelops everything we know, like a snowy day. It's brutal and oppressive, bullying you into not speaking up for fear of losing your loved ones, or job, or flat. It scares you into silencing yourself: you don't get the privilege of speaking honestly about your feelings without extensively assessing the consequences. I have spent a lot of time biting my tongue so hard it might fall off.

And of course, challenging it can have implications on your quality of life. You might lose out on job offers because you've spoken openly and honestly about your experiences and perception of racism online. Interviewing for an admin job a few years ago, I was confronted by a potential colleague about something I'd tweeted about race. Considering it was such a low-ranking position, I didn't think such an intervention was necessary. White privilege is deviously, throat-stranglingly clever, because it owns the companies that recruit you, owns the industries you want to enter, so that if you need money to live you're forced to appease its needs (I locked my Twitter account after that incident, and didn't let any conversations go beyond small talk in all other jobs). It eases you into letting your guard down with white people, assured that you'll be taken seriously, but simultaneously not being surprised when a conversation highlights your difference against your white peers. White privilege is the perverse situation of feeling more comfortable with openly racist, far-right extremists, because at least you know where you stand with them; the boundaries are clear.

The insidious stuff is much harder. You come to expect it, but you can never come to accept it. You learn to be careful about your battles, because otherwise people would consider you to be angry for no reason at all. A troublemaker, not worth taking seriously, an angry black woman obsessed with race.

Back in January 2012 – a mere two days after two of Stephen Lawrence's killers had been sentenced to life imprisonment – somewhat of a Twitter storm was circling around one of Britain's few black female Members of Parliament. In a conversation on Twitter, Diane Abbott, MP for Hackney North and Stoke Newington, was exchanging thoughts on media coverage around the verdict with journalist Bim Adewunmi. It took just one tweet to inadvertently spark one of the biggest furores regarding racism against white people in the UK's recent history. Writing in the *Guardian*, Bim explained the situation.[2] 'In the course of tweeting the events around the trial, conviction and sentencing of Gary Dobson and David Norris for the murder of Stephen Lawrence, I wrote: "I do wish everyone would stop saying 'the black community' though." I expanded in a follow-up: "Clarifying my 'black community' tweet: I hate the generally lazy thinking behind the use of the term. Same for 'black community leaders'." This led to a reply from my local MP Diane Abbott, in which she said: "I understand the cultural point you are making. But you are playing into a 'divide and rule' agenda." We went back and forth for a few tweets more and then Abbott sent out the tweet that caused the furore: "White people love playing 'divide & rule'. We should not play their game #tacticasoldascolonialism."'

At this point, all hell broke loose. The news agenda swiftly changed. No longer were the newspaper editorials, radio packages and TV newspeople discussing Stephen Lawrence, the nuances of institutional racism, or the realities and fears of growing up black in the UK. Now the news story was about racism against white people. Racism goes both ways, Abbott's detractors insisted. Writing in the *Daily Telegraph*, journalist Toby Young wrote: 'imagine the uproar if an equally prominent white Conservative MP said something similar about black people on Twitter?'[3] Even Diane's

Labour Party allies while defending her couldn't help but describe her tone as 'robust and combative',[4] as if their problem was with the tone of her tweet, rather than the injustice it was confronting. And while Britain's white conservatives were insisting that this was 'reverse racism' that was as unforgivable as murdering an unarmed black teenager, Britain's white liberals were terribly concerned that Abbott's harsh phrasing might undo all of her hard work, insisting that adding the word 'some' to her tweet might have softened the impact of it.

Some white people, all white people, or none – it wouldn't have mattered in the end. The aim of these commentators – whether they knew it or not – wasn't to have an honest discussion about British racism. It was to obscure, to derail, and to ardently avoid the wider issue. When it comes to looking at the numbers in the UK's bastions of influence – those that shape national politics and set political agendas – the conclusions to be drawn are clear. The official numbers from the House of Commons show that 94 per cent of Members of Parliament are white.[5] The visible difference of Diane Abbott, one of the few black women in Parliament, who said something very much outside the realm of white agreeableness, is glaringly obvious. She paid the price for rocking the boat.

That the news cycle changed so suddenly, though, was not about the imagined horrors of racism against white people. This multipronged takedown of one of Britain's most prominent black MPs was much more cynical. This was about what academics Alana Lentin and Gavin Titley call 'white victimhood':[6] an effort by the powers that be to divert conversations about the effects of structural racism in order to shield whiteness from much-needed rigorous criticism. The Stephen Lawrence trial was perhaps the closest Britain has ever come to a national conversation on the insidious nature of structural racism, and how it manifests as a collective mindset – partly through malice, partly through carelessness and ignorance – to quietly assist some, while hindering others. But by flipping the debate to one that focused solely on racism against white people, that national conversation was swiftly stopped. No longer was there potential for us as a nation to examine the impact of the legacy of Britain's racism. Instead, we were reminded by lots of very important people that racism goes both ways. In snatching away the possibility of a long overdue conversation, the resulting warped debate revealed an obsession with stopping discussion about race in Britain. The effect was as old as colonialism.

Pointing out how this country has wielded divide and rule as a political strategy is then considered an attack on the very fabric of British sensibilities. The backlash against Diane Abbott wasn't about defending an embattled group of people who are constantly maligned in the media we consume every day. Instead, this reverse-racism row was about the British press closing ranks around what was in its interests to protect – whiteness as a faux neutral, objective power. Whiteness in the press had positioned itself for too long as the self-appointed, self-referential arbiter of racial problems, in which it pondered why these black and brown communities were so prone to violence and poverty, without a shred of self-awareness.

In 2012, the conviction of two of Stephen Lawrence's murderers could have sparked a national conversation about race. We could have had a conversation about the police's failure of Stephen's family as they fought for justice (in 2016, the results from an investigation by the Independent Police Complaints Commission found that while the police were bungling the investigation, an undercover officer was spying on the Lawrence family).[7] We could have asked ourselves honestly, as a country, if taking two decades to convict just two of the gang who murdered an innocent teenager was acceptable. We could have asked ourselves if we were ashamed of that. Maybe we could have spoken about the fact that racism had only been a political priority for less than half a century. We could have had a conversation about riots and race, about accountability, about how to move forward from Britain's most famous race case. We could have had a conversation about how to start eliminating racism. We could have started asking each other about the best way to heal. It could have been pivotal. Instead, the conversation we had was about racism against white people.

Racism does not go both ways. There are unique forms of discrimination that are backed up by entitlement, assertion and, most importantly, supported by a structural power strong enough to scare you into complying with the demands of the status quo. We have to recognise this.

In theory, nobody has a problem with anti-racism. In practice, as soon as people start *doing* anti-racist things, there is no end to the slew of commentators who are convinced anti-racists are doing it wrong. It even happens among people who consider themselves to be progressive.

In the *Weekly Worker* in 2014, socialist writer Charlie Winstanley wrote of his utter disdain at an argument about race that had taken place in his activist group. 'As such,' he wrote, 'oppressed groups sit at the centre of every discussion, backed by the unquestionable moral weight of their subjective life experience, reinforced by an unaccountable structure of etiquette, which they can use to totally control the flow of discourse.'

He continued: 'The total effect is to create an environment in which free discussion of ideas is impossible. Oppressed groups and individuals operate as a form of unassailable priesthood, basing their legitimacy on the doctrine of original sin. To extend the analogy, discussions become confessionals in which participants are encouraged to self-flagellate and prostrate themselves before the holy writ of self-awareness. Shame and self-deprecation are encouraged to keep non-oppressed groups in their place, and subvert the social pyramid of oppression, with oppressed groups at the top.'[8]

Upset by conversations about white privilege that were happening at the time, left-wing writers drew the conclusion that those affected by racism were actually the most privileged, because talking about the effects of racism somehow gave them the moral high ground. This left-wing writer was angrier at people's reactions to racism than the racism itself. This was the beginning of a backlash against conversations about white privilege.

If a person living under the weight of racism wanted to discuss the issues with like-minded people, they might form a group for that purpose. They might opt to call that group a safe space. The concept of a safe space isn't too outlandish. When it comes to race, it could be anywhere that you felt safe enough to discuss your frustrations about the whiteness of the world without fear of being ostracised. It might be a specific moment in your living room with a relative, over lunch with a close colleague, or in a specially convened activist space. But in the middle of a backlash against any and all anti-racist organising, the phrase 'safe space' became another target for white privilege's rage.

'Safe spaces is a direct corollary of the rise of identity politics,' wrote Ian Dunt in the *Guardian*. 'As the essentially economic argument between right and left died down, it was replaced by a culture war in which gender, sexuality and race were at the heart of the discussion.'

'This is the work of privileged, moneyed, over-educated, pampered, middle-class liberal idiots,' added feminist writer Julie Bindel in the same article.[9]

I have often had white people get in touch with me, using the words of civil rights leader Martin Luther King, Jr in attempts to prove to me that my work is misguided, that I am doing it wrong. In emails and tweets, I'm told that Martin Luther King, Jr wanted a world in which people were judged not on the colour of their skin, but the content of their character. The intent of these messages suggests to me that these well-wishers believe that, in today's context, these words are best suited to mean that *white* people should not be judged on the colour of their skin. That the power of whiteness as a race should not be judged. What those who get in touch with me don't seem to realise though, is that, published in the June 1963 issue of *Liberation Magazine* and written from a prison cell in Birmingham, Alabama, Martin Luther King, Jr also mused:

'First, I must confess that over the last few years I have been gravely disappointed with the white moderate. I have almost reached the regrettable conclusion that the Negro's great stumbling block in the stride toward freedom is not the White Citizen's Counciler or the Ku Klux Klanner, but the white moderate who is more devoted to "order" than to justice; who prefers a negative peace which is the absence of tension to a positive peace which is the presence of justice; who constantly says "I agree with you in the goal you seek, but I can't agree with your methods of direct action"; who paternalistically feels he can set the timetable for another man's freedom; who lives by the myth of time and who constantly advises the Negro to wait until a "more convenient season."

'Shallow understanding from people of goodwill is more frustrating than absolute misunderstanding from people of ill will. Lukewarm acceptance is much more bewildering than outright rejection.'[10]

In February 2014, political magazine *The Economist* published an excited editorial on the rise of mixed-race Britain. Using census data, the piece took an in-depth look at trends across the UK pertaining to mixed-race children. Mixed-race people were the fastest-growing ethnic group in Britain since 2001, the magazine wrote, with 6 per cent of children under the age of five identified as mixed race, a higher number than any other black and ethnic minority group in the country. 'For the young,' the article concluded, 'who are used to having people of all backgrounds in their midst, race already matters far less than it did for their parents. In a generation or two more of the melting pot, it may not matter at all.'[11]

In Britain's biggest cities, mixed-race friendships and relationships are now routine rather than controversial. But an increasingly mixed-race Britain makes race relations more complicated, not less. Although nowadays people are much less afraid of living with and loving each other, the problems of racism aren't going to go away. Despite all of the joys and teachable moments of living cheek to cheek, mixed-race children are not going to end racism through their mere existence. White privilege is never more pronounced than in our intimate relationships, our close friendships and our families.

Race consciousness is not contagious, nor is it inherited. If anything, an increase in mixed-race families and mixed-race children brings those difficult conversations about race and whiteness and privilege closer to home (literally) than ever before. No longer can the injustice be quietly ignored by switching off the news or closing the front door.

Talking to Jessica, who is mixed race, is enlightening. We spoke at length about white privilege and family, and the messy, sometimes deeply painful, nature of talking about race with your nearest and dearest. Because of the sensitive nature of our conversation – and the fact that she still has to maintain these relationships – I've changed her name for the purposes of this book.

'These are difficult conversations to have. It's quite raw,' she says. 'I've grown up mainly around my white family. The black side of my family has been affected by domestic violence, which has affected how involved that side of my family has been. For the majority of my thirty years, until the age of twenty-eight, I just didn't talk about race with my white family. My mum's white and my dad's black, and really both my mum and my dad have brought me up in a kind of colour-blind way.'

Unlike me, Jessica can't choose to just stop talking to white people about race. She doesn't have the option of desensitising herself from these discussions, because her mum, and half of her extended family, is white.

'As I've grown older and I understand race a bit more as a mixed-race woman – I identify as black – I've not been prepared for things as a mixed-race woman out in the world,' explains Jessica. 'Now, I've started to have conversations about race with my family. It's uncomfortable because I think they just avoided it. [When I was younger] they pretended like it wasn't an issue. When I've been talking to my mum about it, she said she never thought it was an issue, because I never seemed to have any problems growing up. There were never any racist incidents. And I was like, yes, but racism is more than a one-off incident. It's about the world you live in, and the way you experience your environment.

'Throughout my childhood and throughout my early adult life I've had a feeling of being different, and a bit strange. I could never quite understand why I felt out of place. Now that I'm older and I understand things, I think it was about race. Being the only black child in my class, living in a white town, being surrounded by white family.'

I asked Jessica about some of the difficult conversations she's been having. 'Recently,' she replied, 'my uncle and my cousin have been quite . . . well, they've been really racist. Sharing things on Facebook, sharing Britain First stuff, sharing stuff about "ban the burqa". I've been trying to have conversations with them about why that's racist and why that's hurtful to me as well, and [I'm] just not getting anywhere. They see me talking about race as if I'm a problem, as if I'm a troublemaker. It's caused me to distance myself over the last couple of years from my white family. I don't really see them any more. I couldn't deal with them not understanding where I'm coming from.'

Later, she confides, 'As I've become more conscious in terms of race and where I am in the world, they've become more distant. I know that they are uncomfortable with me, and my sister feels that as well. The more I've become myself, the less comfortable they feel around me. It's really sad, because we used to be a very close family, but I just avoid family get-togethers now.'

Extended family can be avoided. But what about one of the closest relationships in a person's life – what about her relationship with her mother? 'She does get a bit defensive,' says Jessica. 'She's said to me: "I feel like you're forgetting that you're white as well." And I was like "Yeah, Mum, but when I walk down the street, people see a black woman." I experience myself as a black woman. It's hard with our relationship, because I love her, and I want her to accept me, but also she does come out with stuff that's racist . . . That's very painful. My mum, she's completely blinded by her whiteness a lot of the time . . . She just thinks "I can't believe someone can be that biased." She can't imagine institutional bias. So you have to start with the basics. I can't do that with all my family, you know?'

One of Jessica's mum's comments was about her Jamaican dad, and it played into racial stereotypes. 'I remember once she made a comment about black men, and the size of their penises, and how it was true, because of my dad. I was like, Mum, you don't know how fucked up [saying] that is.'

'I feel a lot of love for my mum,' Jessica says with certainty. 'We have a very close relationship, we speak to each other all the time. But she does make me angry when she doesn't understand things. She's making small moves, but in the past, I've had to protect her from my anger. I'm torn. Can I speak my truth to my mum? Even after she's said something, I feel like I couldn't get angry with her. But then weeks after I feel like calling her up and starting an argument about something, to get my anger out. I have to divert the rage to something else.

'I've had a lot of anger. My family just didn't consider what my needs would be as a mixed-race child. My mum and dad, when they got married, it was an issue, because interracial relationships were still controversial, I think. When they got married about thirty-five years ago, they did lose friends. So why didn't they think: "Well, what's this mixed-race child going to experience?" They never did anything to address my cultural needs, so things like how to do my hair, things like Jamaican food, you know, all that stuff that I think is integral to growing up and knowing where you're from.'

Jessica tells me that she is currently in counselling, and has sought out local groups comprised of mixed-race people who have had similar experiences. 'I've had these feelings about my identity and I've just pushed them down, deep down, and I do think they have affected my mental well-being. I have quite a few friends with white mothers who struggle as well. [White] mothers who are using the N word, and say-ing it's fine because they have black children. Now, when I see an interracial couple, I feel uneasy, even though I'm in an interracial relationship. When I see a white parent with a mixed-race kid, I think "Is that child going to get what they need?" Because I didn't get what I needed. I think, for white people who are in interracial relationships, or have mixed-race children, or who adopt transracially, the only way that it will work is if they're actually committed to being anti-racist. To be humble, and to learn that they are racist even if they don't think that they are.'

Of her partner, she says, 'He knows what I've been through. We want children together, and he is the kind of white person who will do that unlearning and unpicking. I only have a few white people in my life like that, and I couldn't be in a relationship with a white person who wasn't. The conversation about race in this country is very limited, and the conversation about mixed-race people in the country is very limited. There are people thinking that you're half and half, that you can only ever be stuck between two worlds. I used to worry about not being black enough, but I'm starting to feel that I'm part of the diversity of blackness. There's more than one way of being black.'

Jessica and her mother's relationship is nuanced, at once deeply loving and deeply painful. It speaks to a number of complexities about racism – showing a truth that is often left out in clunky media coverage – that it is not enacted by malicious monsters driven by ill will, but that it happens by way of whiteness. Rather than mixed-race relationships proving that society is over race, they prove that people's actions often move faster than social progress.

It makes sense that interracial couples might not want to burden themselves with the depressing weight of racial history when planning their lives together, but a colour-blind approach makes life difficult for children who don't deserve this carelessness. It seems that in the same way long-term couples might discuss marriage, money and children, couples of different heritage must discuss race – what it means to them, how it currently affects their lives, and how it might affect their future children's lives.

In among the 'ending racism' confetti being strewn upon mixed-race families is the suspicious eye of busy-bodies who can't quite understand the set-up. Our demographics are changing faster than our attitudes, and it is causing confusion. Anecdotally, I hear from adult children of other mixed-race families who tell me that as children, they've been stopped and questioned in the street when out with their parents, and have endured insults and slurs when their family is travelling out as a group, the tamest being 'rainbow family'.

And there is very little talk of white privilege in transracial adoption – when children of colour are adopted by white families. In 2010, journalist Joseph Harker wrote: 'My own Nigerian father abandoned my Irish mother before I was born. Three years later she married an English local, who later adopted me, and I took his name. I was never short of love, support and encouragement. But when race regularly collided with my life I was ill prepared. I found it difficult to cope with the playground and classroom taunts and, as I grew older, the disconnect with my African heritage became more of an issue. I've spoken to many black people of similar upbringing and they often talk of the same experiences.'[12]

His words strike at the heart of the issue. There's nothing to suggest that a black child with a white parent, or who is adopted into a white family, won't be on the receiving end of immeasurable love and support. But, having never experienced it, the parents might not be well equipped to deal with the racism their child will receive.

In 2012, in the ultimate act of colour-blindness, former Prime Minister David Cameron laid out his plans to remove the legal requirement for local authorities to consider a child's racial, cultural and linguistic background during the adoption process. The move was not without goodwill. In 2013, the Department for Education told the press that black and ethnic minority children are adopted, on average, a year later than their white counterparts. The longer a child is in care, the more likely it is that he or she will develop attachment problems later in life, they said, so finding a good family fit with speed is critical. 'If there is a loving family ready and able to adopt a child,' said the then education secretary Michael Gove, 'issues of ethnicity must not stand in the way.'[13]

It was with a cunning linguistic sleight of hand that the politicians insisted that considering a child's race was actually fuelling racism, with Gove's remarks implying that the fact that black children waiting much longer to be adopted was because of politically correct 'barriers' that (Cameron branded) 'state multiculturalism' had put in place, rather than systemic racism. Why black children wait longer to be adopted is not something easily explained. But we do live in a world riddled with racism, and these waits indicate another blow to a black child's life chances.

Meanwhile, white parents who adopt children of colour take on a new responsibility to be race aware. They embark on a very new journey of self-discovery, and they have a duty to no longer commit to the limiting politics of colour-blindness. They have this duty because a black child cannot be burdened with the responsibility of weathering the world's prejudices on their own. Not all white parents take the time to learn. Sadly, I've met white parents of mixed-race children who have angrily confronted me, insisting that they 'just don't see' race, and telling me that what I'm doing isn't helping at all. Of course, I don't demand that they agree with every point I make, but I do think that it is important that they recognise that we are still living in a racist society, if only so they can counsel their children with some ease. Not for their sake, but for their kids' sake. I really believe that it is the least they can do. On the flip side, I have also met white parents of mixed-race kids who express a real eagerness to understand what their child will face. These are efforts to bridge an information gap that white people don't often have to make. Pretending that everything is fine helps no one.

Despite the title of this book, I knew I couldn't write about race without speaking to at least one white person who thinks about race as much as I do. Jennifer Krase is an American, but has lived in the UK for the last seven years. She is a white immigrant in Britain, which makes her both an outsider and insider: an outsider because her country has its own culture, and its own well-documented racism, and an insider because her white American-ness will have her positioned as an 'expat' rather than an 'immigrant'. She is refreshingly self-aware about all of this. 'I think white people get defensive when you call them white,' she tells me over Skype, 'because they've internalised a message that goes it's rude to point out somebody else's race, and it's dangerous territory because you might inadvertently be racist, because they could take offence at that mention of race. There's a really bizarre circuitous logic that doesn't touch on any of the underlying issues.'

I asked about her early conceptions of racism as she navigated the world as a white child. Being white, Jenny would have probably gone to a school where she was among other white children. And although children always find something to bully each other about, being white, Jenny won't have experienced racism in the playground. 'Originally,' she says, 'I just thought you shouldn't use certain words. Colour-blindness was something that was definitely taught to us in school.

'Growing up, I would have told you that racism is about calling people slurs. Or that racism was about laws about segregation. Or that racism was a two-way street, that anyone can be racist. I probably would have said that words like the N word were worse than someone calling somebody a cracker, for example, but I would have said that cracker is still racist. Now, that sounds ridiculous to me, but that was my very simplistic understanding. That racism was individuals, and I would not have seen systemic things.'

Jenny grew up in the town of Fort Worth in the state of Texas. I asked her about when she became peripherally aware of race in her life. 'Race was something I was always aware of, just not in relation to myself,' she said. 'I thought race was something that applied to other people. Other people who were not white, basically.' Texas, she says, 'has always been a racially charged environment . . . there's always been racial divides between English and non-English speaking people, Latinos. Fort Worth is a very divided city, not only in terms of geography but also life outcomes for people.'

Everything about her heavily monoracial upbringing was comfortably calculated, Jenny explained. 'I lived a really deliberately sheltered existence on a lot of fronts. Not only living, I guess deliberately, around other white people and white communities – my school that I went to was majority white – it was also a fairly middle-class school. The neighbourhoods around the school at the time were fairly affluent. There were all these different factors that led to me being in a very specific environment. I don't think any of that was accidental. My parents buying a house – you look at the neighbourhoods and you look at the schools, and you make decisions based on your own criteria, some of which may be overtly racist, or classist. "I want my kid to have a good school." What does a good school mean?'

Given her background, I wondered how her stance on race could so drastically change from then to now. In my experience, a white person who has had an almost all-white upbringing brings with them an insularity, as well as a reflexive urge to defend whiteness when it is criticised. At what point in her life did she first realise she was white? '[I had a lecturer whose] class was unbelievably challenging for me, because he talked about race. He talked about race, he talked about imperialism . . . That was my first exposure, not just to the facts of it, but to politically challenging historical viewpoints on it. At the time I was really resistant to it. Thinking back to what I said now, and I just fucking cringe at it. But that really planted the seeds of change for me.'

At first, she was defensive. 'I think what made me feel defensive is that I was embarrassed that there was a chance that someone knew something that I didn't. On some level, maybe I could sense that accepting whatever that person was saying would open a can of worms. It was a combination of embarrassment and panic. I can't put my finger on exactly what I was trying to protect or defend. I think it was an indignation.

'I've lost a lot of sensitivity about being told I'm wrong. That's a massive gain, on a personal level. I haven't lost my white privilege. It hasn't reduced because I suddenly understand what it is.'

I was curious to learn how Jenny's anti-racist politics affected the rest of her life. 'I discuss [racism] with family, with friends, in a work context, although those discussions can be really difficult,' she says. 'In the last three or four years, I've definitely had a few mega-fails where that is concerned, where I've either picked the wrong discussion to have or passed up the chance to have a discussion that was essential.

'I'm trying to do more things in my ordinary day-to-day life that aren't in activist spaces, to bring issues up when they're relevant at that time. Because I don't know what the other people in the room are thinking, but if I'm thinking about that and no one else is saying it, then it's on me to say something. Being accountable for that, really only to myself. Doing things when there's nobody there to see it, because it's not really about somebody witnessing it or patting me on the back for it.'

It is unusual that Jenny is willing to do the heavy work of dismantling racism. Frankly, it's unusual because she is white. So many white people think that racism is not their problem. But white privilege is instrumental to racism. When I write about white people in this book, I don't mean every individual white person. I mean whiteness as a political ideology. A school of thought that favours whiteness at the expense of those who aren't. To me, it is like yin and yang. Racism's legacy does not exist without purpose. It brings with it not just a disempowerment for those affected by it, but an empowerment for those who are not. That is white privilege. Racism bolsters white people's life chances. It affords an unearned power; it is designed to maintain a quiet dominance. Why don't white people think they have a racial identity?

4

Fear of a Black Planet

In 1968, the late Conservative politician Enoch Powell told a rapt audience in a speech about the ills of immigration: 'In this country in fifteen or twenty years' time, the black man will have the whip hand over the white man.'[1] Inadvertently, he revealed his own tacit recognition of racist power relations in the country at the time, and although he didn't explicitly say it (because he knew what side he was on), Powell clearly thought that a power transfer in race relations would lead to white British people facing the mistreatment and systemic barriers that black people were working to overcome. There is a reason why he said 'whip hand over' rather than using the less symbolic phrasing 'advantage over'. Whip conjures images of beatings, misery and forced labour, of subjugation and total dominance – of slavery. Enoch Powell's speech has consistently been earmarked as one of the most racist speeches in British history, but his language was only as racially charged as Britain's relationship with blackness has historically been. The only way he could envision power being maintained in Britain was by subjugation of a people, because that is how Britain has held and maintained its power in the past.

The projection of an ever-encroaching black dooms-day is what I call 'fear of a black planet'. It's a fear that the alienated 'other' will take over. Enoch Powell's fears of a flipped script have lived on in modern-day political rhetoric on immigration. When, in the run-up to the 2015 general election, the Labour Party released official merchandise which included a mug that read 'controls on immigration', they played into that fear. Some insist that we are living on a tiny island and it's time to shut the doors. There is a worry the ever-disappearing essence of Britishness is being slowly eroded by immigrants whose sole interest is not to flee from war or poverty, but to destroy the social fabric of the country.

The fear takes on many guises. We hear it in the form of 'concerns about' immigration, touted by polit-ical parties in recent general elections. We hear it in the form of 'preserving our national identity'. At the core of the fear is the belief that anything that doesn't represent white homogeneity exists only to erase it. That multiculturalism is the start of a slippery slope towards the destruction of Western civilisation.

It seemed borderline paranoid when UKIP's Nigel Farage[2] expressed a nervousness at hearing fellow pas-sengers speak different languages in his train carriage.

In a 2014 speech, he said, 'The fact [is] that in scores of our cities and market towns, this country in a short space of time has frankly become unrecognisable. Whether it is the impact on local schools and hospitals, whether it is the fact in many parts of England you don't hear English spoken any more. This is not the kind of community we want to leave to our children and grandchildren.'[3]

Decades after Enoch Powell's speech, and the fear of a black planet has in no way subsided. The word multiculturalism has become a proxy for a ton of British anxieties about immigration, race, difference, crime and danger. It's now a dirty word, a front word for fears about black and brown and foreign people posing a danger to white Brits. If you are an immigrant – even if you're second or third generation – this is personal. You *are* multiculturalism. People who are scared of multiculturalism are scared of *you*. And, in the spirit of 1980s-style political blackness, 'immigration concerns' are less about who is black, and more about who *isn't* white British.

In campaign literature for the referendum on Britain's membership of the EU, the Vote Leave campaign wrote that 'there were 475,000 live births to mothers from other EU countries between 2005 and 2014, the equivalent of adding a city the size of Manchester to the population.'[4] This was cloaked in a conversation about the 'strain' immigrants put

119

on the NHS, but I've heard this discussion before. In the US, the phrase 'anchor baby' is used in the pejorative sense to admonish US-born children of immigrants. It suggests a takeover. Britain is not innocent of this kind of punitive talk. In 2016, one hospital began considering passport checks for non-emergency patients – including pregnant women – before they received treatment.[5] In more campaign literature before the referendum, posters from UKIP read: 'We want our country back: Vote to Leave'.[6] The last time I heard the slogan 'we want our country back' was in my university town, when far-right group the English Defence League were staging a protest about what they called the 'Islamification' of Britain. Now, another form of the phrase – 'taking our country back' – is used as a strapline by Britain First. An IPSOS Mori poll published days before the EU referendum vote confirmed that immigration was the top issue for would-be leave voters.[7] What was once fringe is now mainstream.

This is nothing new. For a long time now, far-right political groups have hijacked the anti-colonial struggles of native people in America and Australia to create a story of the embattled indigenous white British, under siege from immigration. Around the same time the English Defence League were marching through my university town, a group of my friends crowded into my student bedroom to watch former British

National Party leader Nick Griffin on BBC *Question Time*. I watched in disbelief as he said: 'No one here would dare go to New Zealand and say to a Maori "what do you mean indigenous?" You wouldn't dare go to North America and say to an American Red Indian "what do you mean indigenous? We're all the same."' He continued: 'The indigenous people of these islands, the English, the Scots, the Irish and the Welsh . . . it's the people who have been here overwhelmingly for the last 17,000 years. We are the aboriginals here . . . The simple fact is that the majority of the British people are descended from people who've lived here since time immemorial. It's extraordinarily racist, it is genuinely racist when you seek to deny the English. You people wouldn't even let us have our name on the census form. That is racism. And that's why people are voting British National Party.'

It seemed to be that for Nick Griffin, accommodating difference was akin to erasing white Britishness. The comfort of white privilege blinds him to the fact that he is part of the majority and that he is *already catered for*. In his *Question Time* monologue, Griffin appealed to that British sense of fairness to conjure images of an embattled white minority under attack, losing control of their heritage and culture. Even more insultingly, he used the struggles of black and brown people who were colonised, raped and beaten by white British people to preserve white British culture.

Because of British defamation laws, you can get into hot water if you publish something that harshly criticises someone without giving them the right to reply in the same piece of work. I think that a book detailing British racism would be remiss to overlook the vast influence Nick Griffin and the British National Party has had in how we talk about race today. So I found myself in the position of trying to get in contact with Nick Griffin, a man who, throughout my lifetime, has openly attacked the idea of people like me being *truly* British, and who represented a party that held policies stating that my mixed-race family is an abomination.

Having been in the same position a few years before me, an editor I work with gave me his address. I wrote Mr Griffin a letter. He replied the next day, agreeing to speak to me. I suggested meeting at my publisher's offices. He declined, saying he hardly ever goes to London, as it's 'largely a foreign country'. We agreed to speak on the phone the next day.

I was very worried throughout this whole process, but I chose to use my own mobile number to call him, in an effort to be as open and honest as possible. I needed the interview, after all, and acting suspicious or withholding information was not going to help with that. But I'd handed over my personal phone number to one of the most infamous British far-right leaders in the last fifty years. If he so wished, he could make my life a living hell with a few keystrokes. He could choose to post my number online. I knew it was something he'd done before – posting the address of a gay couple online back in 2012.[8] My only security was that we both had something over each other – I had his number and email address. So I took the risk. Our conversation was so surreal that I publish it here in full.

REL: Back in 2009, you said something along the lines that white British people are an ethnic minority in Britain. Do you still think that?
NG: Not are. Will become.

Why do you think white people will become an ethnic minority in Britain, then?
It's simply a demographic fact. If you want to go and look, I'd look at Professor Coleman from Oxford University. He's probably Britain's leading demographer. Using government figures, not my figures, he said some years ago we'd be a minority in our own country by the end of this century at the latest. That was at present trends, but of course, present trends have got worse. So there's simply no doubt about it. Not just Britain, but the whole of Western Europe.

But currently in Britain, 81.9 per cent of the population is white British, don't you think that's a bit far-fetched?

No, that's how demographics works. The British population is very large compared to the others, you're right. But if you look at the age differences between the populations, and the British population is significantly made up of two waves of baby boomers who, over the next twenty years, are going to die off at an incredible rate . . . It's going to go up. Whereas the age profile of a number of the immigrant populations is much younger, therefore they'll have more children. You're not arguing with me, you need to go and argue with Professor Coleman. He's a leading demographer in the world, and you and I aren't. What he says is true. There's really no doubt about it.

Why do you think that his projections are bad news, then?
I regard that as a racist question. Because no white person would dare to go to, say, Nigeria, if Nigeria was being flooded with Chinese, and say 'Why do you think it's a bad idea that Nigeria should cease to be Nigeria?' It's self-evident that all the peoples of the world have a right to remain the dominant people, culturally and ethnically, in their own homeland. Anyone who says otherwise, just because we happen to be Europeans, is a racist.

I see. So I'm a racist then.
No, no, I'm not saying you're a racist. It's in saying that, with that point of view. [If you're happy to] have

fewer rights than Nigerians, then you're a racist. If you'd be absolutely happy for Nigerians to become Chinese, then you're not a racist, you're just mad.

This was many years ago, so please do clarify for me, [but] is it true that the BNP had a policy, or had some sort of statement on the website, saying no to mixed-race relationships?
Yes.

Is that an idea that you share?
I think that it's unfortunate when people are wiped out by a vast amount of racial integration. Muhammad Ali said exactly the same thing. I think that either nature or God made people separate, unique and wonderful, all of them, then it's a shame if we're all simply obliterated into one indistinguishable mass all over the world. It's a pity. Having said which, it's not for any state to determine who falls in love with who.

So do you think that the white British population is under attack from immigration and mixed-race relationships?
I think that the identity of all the peoples of Europe is under threat from mass immigration, integration, and mixed-race relationships, which aren't in fact happening just because it's a natural thing, but because they're constantly promoted by every element of the

mass media as a good thing. It's a deliberate policy, it's very very clear. If you go back to Coudenhove-Kalergi, the man who founded the European Union, he was openly saying in 1926 that the idea [was to] obliterate the nations of Europe in constitutional terms but also the peoples who made them. Through mass immigration and mass assimilation. Socially engineered assimilation, that's what's happening. We're under attack. Not by immigrants, but by an elite who want to use immigrations to obliterate the nations of Europe.

I'm pretty sure it was British government policy, particularly in the post-war period, to actually bring over people from the Commonwealth for labour reasons. Don't you think it's a bit disingenuous to suggest that these people who sometimes have been asked, and sometimes have been ruled by Britain . . . if they come over to get their piece of the pie, why is that unfair?

It's wrong because of the effect it has on Britain. I'm not blaming the immigrants. You're quite right, if the government support them, if senior civil servants have encouraged people. It's the people who control the mass media, the big corporations, big business that wants cheap labour, to undermine the power of organised unionised labour. They're the people to blame, not the immigrants.

Why do you pinpoint mass media when a lot of our media in Britain – I mean it's owned by a few people, you're right there – but we have a lot of tabloid media that is quite explicitly anti-immigration.

We do indeed. It's explicitly anti-immigration. But it generally happily goes along with the genocidal implications of mass immigration. So it's certainly not a nationalist media. And in terms of the media that really influences how people think and what they do, there is no comparison between print media, and what people see. It's the power of the Hollywood films, it's the power of the television news, particularly the power of the soap operas. These are the things which are particularly effective at changing how people view the world and what they do. A newspaper, however it reports the news, is in print. It doesn't have anything like the power of the broadcast media. It's the fact that the broadcast media, run by a tiny handful of people and directed by a very small interest group that all want the same thing, they're the ones who really have the effect. Forget the *Daily Mail*, it's the soap operas that decide how people work in their heads.

When you say they all want the same thing, what is it that you think they want? Because I work in the media, and it's very white – British journalism is something like 96 per cent white. These newsrooms and places are not particularly multicultural.

No, no, no, they're not, but they're part of the hypocrisy of the liberal elite. They want the ordinary working class to enjoy the tremendous diversity and benefits of mass immigration that goes with it. But they don't want it for themselves, do they? They don't want it for their kids. The Rupert Murdochs of this world want power and they want wealth, and they don't want anyone to challenge it. The whole corporate, the 1 per cent around the world, they are well aware they are looting our public services, the resources. It used to be that colonialism and the looting was done by the West in the Third World. The looting is now of the corporations of all of us, and they're well aware that sooner or later, any sovereign, any European people that still has its identity intact, they can say we've had enough of the looting, we're taking it all back. So the only way to make sure the looting is permanent is to get rid of the peoples who otherwise would say we're having a revolution.

Do you think that by Britain accommodating difference, people from different races and cultures, that that is akin to erasing white Britishness?
In small numbers, no. But that is the aim and it's the inevitable result of large numbers, yes.

My parents are from a [former] Commonwealth country, and I've got a British passport. Born and raised here. When you say these things, you may pinpoint the elite as spreading an agenda and what not, but it does

tend to make someone like me feel quite unwelcome. There's many, many second-generation immigrants who feel very British.

You're quite young, I would recommend that you get the hell out of this country and you go and have kids somewhere decent, probably somewhere connected with your own heritage, because Britain is, to be crude, utterly fucked.

Nick Griffin is an extreme example, but he voices the same fears that are evident in the low-level grumblings and resentment of some British people who are resistant to change. They spend their time yearning for a nostalgic Britain that never was.

Fear of a black planet maintains that people of colour are unfairly vying for precious, rationed and scarce resources, and that having more people of colour in these positions of power might instigate a drastic tipping of the scales. To some, every time a new curry house opens, every *polski sklep* that opens, and every time Sainsbury's expands its ethnic food aisle, it's a symbol that white Brits are sleepwalking into new minority status. Some start boycotting halal meat on cruelty grounds, as though there are varying degrees of acceptable animal death they'll withstand for the benefit of eating their burgers. Fear of a black planet is a fear of loss.

Another incarnation of the fear reveals a deep-seated discomfort with anti-racist talk and protest. Couched in the pernicious frame of 'freedom of speech', it material-ises when a person with anti-racist values voices their disgust at something racist. They will then be told that their sheer objection to it actually *inhibits* freedom of speech.

Late 2015 saw the rise of a British Rhodes Must Fall movement. Inspired by similar protests from students in South Africa's University of Cape Town, students at Oxford University set their sights on removing a statue of colonial businessman Cecil Rhodes on their university campus. As well as founding mining company De Beers Consolidated Mines (eventually diamond purveyors De Beers), Cecil Rhodes played a key part in expanding the British Empire in South Africa, based on the belief that the British were 'the finest race in the world'. His colonial project dis-placed Africans from their land. The country we now know as Zimbabwe was once named Rhodesia, after Rhodes. The country's citizens attempted to resist British rule, and paid with their lives. For many, Rhodes was the father of South African apartheid. When he lived in Britain, he attended Oxford's Oriel College, and a statue of him still stands there today. It was in 2015 that students studying at the university let it be known loud and clear that they wanted that statue gone.

A national debate about whether the statue should fall ensued. The black student protesters were accused of being undemocratic. 'Cecil Rhodes was a racist,' read one headline, 'but you can't readily expunge him from history.' That was a strange conclusion to draw, because campaigning to take down a statue is not the same as tippexing Cecil Rhodes' name out of the history books. The Rhodes Must Fall campaign was not calling for Rhodes to be erased from history. Instead they were questioning whether he should be so overtly celebrated. The campaign's opponents – who included Lord Patten, the Chancellor of Oxford University – said that by exercising their democratic right to protest, the students were actually impinging on freedom of speech. By making a fuss, disrupting the everyday, and pointing out the problem, they had *become* the problem. Somehow, it wasn't believable that Lord Patten simply wanted free and fair debate and a healthy exchange of ideas on his campus. It looked like he just wanted silence, the kind of strained peace that simmers with resentment, the kind that requires some to suffer so that others are comfortable.

To insist that Rhodes Must Fall campaigners were restricting discussion was simply a lie. The work of the protest movement brought little-known aspects of Britain's colonial involvement in Africa to prime-time news, exposing the facts to audiences who almost certainly wouldn't have learnt about it on the national curriculum. What student protesters achieved was the opposite of shutting down debate. That the campaign was misrepresented revealed the passive-aggressive anti-black sleight of hand that so many British conversations about race are guilty of indulging in.

This 'freedom of speech' fight can hardly even be called a debate. Instead, it is one-sided, with the powerful side constantly warping the terms of engagement. Couching opposition to anti-racist speech and protest as a noble fight for freedom of speech is about protecting white people from being criticised. It seems there is a belief among some white people that being accused of racism is far worse than actual racism. If Rhodes Must Fall's detractors really believed in freedom of speech, they would have let the debate happen without throwing around disingenuous accusations that black people were stopping them from speaking freely. They would have engaged with the ideas being put forward rather than using intellectually dishonest tricks designed to circumvent taking the protesters seriously. I think that there is a fear among many white people that accepting Britain's difficult history with race means somehow admitting defeat.

Rhodes Must Fall was a small-scale example of what racial injustice looks like in Britain. It looks normal. It is pedestrian. It is unquestioned. It's just a part of the landscape, you might walk past it every day.

For people who oppose anti-racism on the grounds of freedom of speech, opposition to gross racial disparities is about 'offence', rather than the heavily unequal material conditions that people affected by it carry as burden. Being in a position where their lives are so comfortable that they don't really have anything material to oppose, faux 'free speech' defenders spend all their spare time railing against 'offence culture'. When they make it about offence rather than their own complicity in a drastically unjust system, they successfully transfer the responsibility of fixing the system from the benefactors of it to those who are likely to lose out because of it. Tackling racism moves from conversations about justice to conversations about sensitivity. Those who are repeatedly struck by racism's tendency to hinder their life chances are told to toughen up and grow a thicker skin.

Free speech is a fundamental foundation of a free and fair democracy. But let's be honest and have the guts to unpick who gets to speak, where, and why. The real test of this country's perimeters of freedom of speech will be found if or when a person can freely discuss racism without being subject to intellectually dishonest attempts to undermine their arguments. If free speech, as so many insist, includes being prepared to hear opinions that you don't like, then let's open up the parameters of what we consider acceptable debate. I don't mean new versions of old bigotry. I mean, that if we have to listen to this kind of bigotry, then let us have the equal and opposite viewpoint. If Katie Hopkins, with help from the *Sun* newspaper, publishes a column describing desperate refugees trying to travel to Britain as cockroaches,[9] then we need a cultural commentator that advocates for true compassion and total open borders. Not the kind of wishy-washy liberalism that harps on about the cultural and economic contributions of migrants to this country as though they are resources to be sucked dry, but someone who speaks in favour of migrants and open borders with the same force of will with which Hopkins despises them.

It's about time that critiques of racism were subject to the same passionate free speech defence as racist statements themselves. Freedom of speech means the freedom for opinions on race to clash. Freedom of speech doesn't mean the right to say what you want without rebuttal, and racist speech and ideas need to be healthily challenged in the public sphere. White fear tries to stop this conversation from happening.

Fear of a black planet exists not just in the real world, but also in the fictional. After four-year-old me came to terms with the fact that I would never turn white, I found refuge in white fictional British and American characters that I could relate to. For so long, that fictional heroic character loved by so many has been assumed to be white, because whiteness has been assumed to be universal. It is in film, television and books that we see the most potent manifestations of white as the default assumption. A character simply cannot be black without a pre-warning for an assumed white audience. Black characters as leads are considered unrelatable (with the exception of a handful of high-profile, crossover black Hollywood stars). When casting for film and TV *does* take the step to cast outside of whiteness, fans repeatedly reveal their ugly side, voicing their upset, disgust and disappointment. Fear of black characters is fear of a black planet.

When Sony Pictures suffered the great email hack of 2014, correspondence from chairwoman Amy Pascal revealed that she was keen on the idea of black actor Idris Elba as the next James Bond. A year later, and artfully coinciding with promotions for his latest book, author Anthony Horowitz ended up apologising for saying that Idris Elba was too 'street' to play the iconic British character. Online, a debate was raging over whether a black Bond could ever be legitimate. That there was such uproar about James Bond, the epitome of slick, suave Britishness, possibly being tainted with just a hint of black, proved again the demarcation lines of what it means to be British. When newspapers covered the 'Idris Elba as Bond' speculation, the comments almost broke the Internet. 'I'd never watch a Bond film again,' cried one *Daily Mail* reader. What were they so scared of? This strength of feeling over classic stories being ruined wasn't around when the Charles Dickens novel *Oliver Twist* was remade into a film in which the lead character was cast in the image of a cartoon cat.

When the seventh *Star Wars* film saw black British actor John Boyega cast as a stormtrooper, a new league of angry people took to social media to call for a boycott of the film, calling it anti-white propaganda. This was because two of the film's heroes were black, and the film's villains were all white. The more extreme corners of the Internet echoed Nick Griffin by insisting that this casting decision was part of a wider cultural project to instigate a white genocide. The fear was intense – and it was linked to wider white nationalist fears about white people becoming a racial minority in the Western world.

In the run-up to Christmas 2015, the Internet was polarised by the prospect of a black Hermione Granger. The lead cast had just been announced for *Harry Potter and the Cursed Child*, a play based on the books, set nineteen years after the seventh book ended. Hermione Granger was to be played by Noma Dumezweni, a black actress of South African heritage. Upon hearing the news, some were ecstatic, but others were outraged. Some fans fixated on a sentence from *Harry Potter and the Prisoner of Azkaban* – 'Hermione's white face was sticking out from behind a tree' – as hard evidence that any deviation from a white actress was sacrilege.

As a child, I was a fully fledged Harry Potter fan, queuing up outside bookshops at midnight for the latest release, and speed-reading the books once I'd got my grubby hands on them so I could know the conclusion before any of my friends. Hermione's race didn't matter so much to me then, but when CBBC's *Newsround* announced open auditions for the main cast, eleven-year-old me grabbed my copy of *The Prisoner of Azkaban* and read out all of Hermione's bits as I paced around the back garden. I didn't end up sending any of my information to the programme, though, because I sort of knew that if the book didn't explicitly say she was black, then she probably wasn't. There would be no point in auditioning for the part.

It was heartening, then, to see J. K. Rowling come out in support of a black Hermione, rebuffing the angry literalists by tweeting that, when it came to the character, 'white skin was never specified'. But when you are used to white being the default, black isn't black unless it is clearly pointed out as so. As an adult Harry Potter fan, I'd begun to think of Hermione Granger, with her house-elf liberation campaign, as a well-meaning but guilty-feeling white liberal, taking on a social justice cause with gusto without ever really consulting the views and feelings of the people she was fighting for. Outside of the wizarding world, Hermione would be working at an NGO or a charity, or slowly climbing the bureaucracy of the United Nations. With her strong moral compass, she'd be educated and adamant about animal rights or global warming.

Far from destroying our most well-loved works of fiction, abandoning assumptions of the whiteness of our characters infinitely expands all of the fictional universes, whether it be the wizarding world or the Star Wars galaxy. As vlogger Rosianna Halse Rojas points out,[10] reading Harry Potter's Hermione as black is a whole different ball game. It brings to light the incredibly racialised language of blood purity used in the wizarding world, of mudbloods and purebloods. This is terminology that could have been easily lifted straight from Nazi Germany or apartheid South Africa. Hermione's parents were muggles after all, and that is how states and scientists have categorised races and fuelled racism – as though some heritages are con-tagious and are spread through lineage and blood. A black or mixed-race Hermione enduring spat-out slurs of 'mudblood' from her peers, plucked from her parents, told she's special and part of a different race altogether, might be very keen to assimilate, to be accepted. No wonder she tried so hard. No wonder she did her friends' homework, and was first to raise her hand in class. She was the model minority. A black or mixed-race Hermione agitating to free house elves, after six or seven years of enduring racial slurs, might not have the courage to challenge her peers, and instead might have hung on to something she felt she really *could* change.

That some Harry Potter fans struggled to imagine a black Hermione meant that they couldn't imagine little black girls as precocious, intelligent, logical know-it-alls with hearts of gold. It's a shame that they couldn't imagine quiet, unassuming black middle-class parents who work as dentists. It's sad that blackness in their heads is stuck in an ever-repetitive script, with strict parameters of how a person should be. The imaginations of black Hermione's detractors can stretch to the possibility of a secret platform at King's Cross station that can only be accessed by running through a brick wall, but they can't stretch to a black central character.

We are told that black actors and actresses cast as central characters in works of fiction are unrealistic. We are told that they are historically inaccurate, or that they are too far a stretch of the imagination. But really, this is about a belligerent section of society that refuses to think outside of themselves, who believe that everything must cater to them and the rest of us must adapt to their whims and wishes. And this is nothing but insulting when heard by the black fiction lover who, if they are to enjoy their chosen genre, have no choice *but* to empathise with a character who looks nothing like them.

This line of thought demonstrates a real struggle to identify with black humanity in any conceivable way. To them we are an unidentifiable shifting mass, a simplistic, animalistic herd. They don't believe that black characters have the capacity to be sophisticated like James Bond, or intelligent like Hermione Granger. But those of us who aren't white have been subjected to having to identify with the lives of white main characters since film began. Fear of a black planet destroys good fiction, and it demonstrates how racism gets in the way of human empathy. Seeing non-white characters relegated to sidekick or token status has been routine for so long that, for some, attempting to try and relate to black skin in a main character is a completely alien concept. We've been positioned as the 'other', only taking centre stage to portray subjugation or provide comic relief. White people are so used to seeing a reflection of themselves in all representations of humanity at all times, that they only notice it when it's taken away from them.

Fear of a black planet manifests in a co-opting of the language of liberation to describe white resentment, anger and discontent. There is talk of fairness, without acknowledging what is already unfair. It manifests in a rigid and shallow understanding of freedom of speech (generally understood to be the final frontier in the fight to be as openly bigoted as possible without repercussions). The fear of a black planet is the by-product of social and demographic change, and calls for state accountability. There is an old saying about the straight man's homophobia being rooted in a fear that gay men will treat him as he treats women. This is no different.

And the fear is completely unfounded. Power and wealth in this country is still concentrated in very few, very white hands, and power never goes down without a fight. Your life chances are still drastically influenced by your race and class. Demographic change might spearhead some representational wins at the top, but we are far from any *Noughts & Crosses*-style black supremacy.[11] Regardless, that isn't the kind of world anti-racists are envisioning when they agitate for justice. It has always been about the redistribution of power rather than the inverting of it.

The paradox, of course, is that those who oppose anti-racism have worked themselves into quite the double bind. It's a bit of a Schrödinger's cat situation. If, as they say, racism doesn't exist, and black people have nothing to complain about, why are they so afraid of white people becoming the new minority? I suppose we will all have to wait in suspense until 2066 – the projected year when white people will be a demographic minority in Britain – to find out.

5

THE FEMINISM QUESTION

Back in October 2012, I sat in a cold university library, furiously typing out a blog post on race and feminism. I was supposed to be revising, but was so irritated I could barely sit still. Lena Dunham's television programme *Girls* had premiered that year to critical acclaim. It was widely regarded as an accurate reflection of young women's lives. The characters were all working low-paid jobs and waiting for their lives to begin. They bickered among themselves, and wrestled with jealousy, pettiness, and body-image troubles. These were all characteristics I recognised among my peers and myself. Most of us were just drudging ahead, balancing unpaid internships alongside bar or retail jobs in the hope that we would reap the same rewards for hard work as the generation before us did. We had been hoping for a nine-to-five job and secure housing. We thought that if we worked hard enough, we would rid ourselves of that panicky feeling that sets in when you don't quite know where next month's rent is coming from. The scenarios in

Girls were hugely familiar. But the programme, set in New York City, was starkly white. Because of this, it was hard to take commentators seriously when they insisted that it was the most feminist television show in decades.

As a result of the show, one of the most prominent debates in recent years about feminism's race problem began to brew. Some asserted that it would be nothing but tokenistic for Dunham to write black characters into her TV show just for the sake of it. Others said that it was absurd to set a television show with an all-white cast in one of the most racially diverse cities in America. To me, it was obvious. It also wasn't really about a TV programme, although the programme was symptomatic of a widespread problem. Finishing up the blog post, I wrote: 'When feminists can see the problem with all-male panels, but can't see the problem with all-white television programmes, it's worth questioning who they're really fighting for.'

On reflection, the representation and inclusion of black faces wasn't actually what I was passionate about. This wasn't about being seen, or about being included. I was used to not seeing positive reflections of black people in popular culture. An all-white television programme was nothing new to me. What I was really upset about was the ease with which white people defended their all-white spaces and spheres. Theirs was an impenetrable bubble, and their feminism sat neatly within it. Not only this, but the feminists who insisted they were agitating for a better world for all women didn't actually give a shit about black people and, by extension, they didn't give a shit about women of colour. Gender equality must be addressed, but race could languish in the corner.

The same sort of scenario happened repeatedly over the next couple of years. Just one year later, pop star Lily Allen released her first music video, 'Hard Out Here', after a long hiatus from the music industry. The formula of the resulting race row was similar to the furore around *Girls*. A young and successful white woman had revealed public work that was immediately lauded as raw, relatable and utterly, thoroughly feminist – the definitive anthem for young women everywhere. In this instance though, it wasn't a lack of black people that sparked upset. The black bodies were present, but Lily Allen's black back-up dancers were scantily clad, dancing in a parody of misogynistic hip-hop videos as she sang about glass ceilings, objectification, and strongly implied that smart girls didn't need to strip to be successful.

After a while, it became wise to stop paying attention to anything tagged vaguely feminist in popular media, as it would only end up being disappointing. What I carried on doing was writing.

On New Year's Eve of 2013, I was invited by a BBC producer to appear on Radio 4's *Woman's Hour*. It was a fairly innocent request – to discuss the year in feminism alongside Laura Bates of the Everyday Sexism Project, and Caroline Criado-Perez, who that year had campaigned to have historical women figures featured on British banknotes. When I took my seat in the studio, I realised I was the only black face in the room. That was the first red flag. I was joined by Laura and the radio presenter. Caroline was phoning in. The segment began. I was nervous. I explained that I didn't really consider myself a campaigner, but that during the year I had been writing about racism in the feminist movement – my frustrations with a doggedly white-centric perspective from the movement's 'leaders' – and found that lots of women who were not white were feeling exactly the same way. 'A tide has turned in terms of these issues in feminism,' I said. 'They cannot be ignored any more.'[1]

The burden then fell on me to explain why feminism was so divided, and why feminism needed a race analysis in the first place. I was asked: 'What lies at the bottom of the divisions, and why has the phrase "check your privilege" become so popular?' That was the second red flag. This framing suggested that racism wasn't a concern for my white peers. Having worked with Laura Bates in the past, I knew that this wasn't the case. Despite my discomfort, I put forward my case for the need for a race analysis in feminism. But my point was quickly picked up on by Caroline Criado-Perez, who said that people had used an anti-racist perspective as a reason to harass and bully her online.

The context of her comment was very disturbing. Earlier in that year, Caroline's women-on-banknotes campaign had drawn national headlines. The press coverage attracted a misogynist sentiment, and what started out as a win quickly descended into one of the most high-profile British cases of online harassment. When the Bank of England announced plans to put an image of the author Jane Austen on the ten-pound note, the women-on-banknotes campaign claimed this as a success. But because of the harassment that followed as a result of the campaign's work, Caroline had been sent death threats. She received messages that told her that bombs had been installed outside of her home. She was repeatedly messaged by anonymous ill-wishers who were encouraging her to commit suicide. Eventually, two people pled guilty to sending her some of the more vicious tweets. They were sentenced to twelve and eight weeks in prison respectively, under the Malicious Communications Act.

On that New Year's Eve *Woman's Hour*, Caroline's comment, aimed at discrediting her online abusers, came across as equating my work and politics with these vicious and abusive messages. I felt implicated in the harassment against her. In the BBC studio, it fell to me to account for Caroline's horrific experiences, putting me in the position of defending the arguments (that I didn't share) of people I didn't even know. I was completely lost for words.

This was the cost of representation. The overwhelming whiteness of feminism – on a radio-show segment that would have been all white if it wasn't for my presence – was not considered a problem. I had wanted to discuss how feminism wasn't exempt from white privilege, but instead I found myself on the receiving end of it.

There was an Internet storm about the interview immediately after we came off air. Some people were as shocked at this assertion as I was. Others were convinced that I was a liar and a bully who had been waging a war against Caroline online – not true – and that by balking at her intervention, I was playing the victim. I hadn't wanted to at first, but after some encouragement from friends, a few hours later I wrote a short blog post clarifying what went on.

Think about the last time you heard a comprehensive description of the nature of structural racism in the mainstream media, I wrote. *These issues just don't get the kind of airtime that feminism does in the UK press. Think hard about the last time you*

heard a person of colour challenge the virulently rac-
ist rhetoric around immigration in this country, or
just state the plain fact that structural racism prevails
because white people are treated more favourably in
the society we live in. I was afforded the opportu-
nity to do this live, on national radio. I didn't take
it lightly.

After a concerted effort from many a white woman
to portray black feminist thought as destructive
and divisive, I'm aware that accepting these media
requests is a double-edged sword. It was Audre
Lorde who said: 'If I didn't define myself for myself,
I would be crunched into other people's fantasies for
me and eaten alive.' Though it sometimes feels like
I am entering into a trap, I'm hyper-aware that if
I don't accept these opportunities, black feminism
will be mischaracterised and misrepresented by the
priorities of the white feminists taking part in the
conversation . . . I'm tired of this tribal deadlock.
I meant what I said on the programme: the only
way to foster any shared solidarity is to learn from
each other's struggles, and recognise the various
privileges and disadvantages that we all enter the
movement with.

Caroline apologised in the early evening, writing on
Twitter: 'I just wanted to apologise if this am it came
across at all like I was suggesting the abuse is something you have been party to. I didn't mean to imply

that at all, but I can see that given I responded to your comment, it might have seemed like that. I didn't want to suggest I have ever felt abused by you – I haven't, because of course you haven't abused me. I just wanted to take the opportunity to talk about abuse I have experienced and how damaging I think it is, because I think it needs to stop. But perhaps could have picked a better moment/way of saying it. So am sorry for that.'

Despite her apology, the day got worse.

The former Conservative MP and self-fashioned right-wing feminist Louise Mensch saw fit to swoop in and support Caroline. She began to tweet at me. 'Reni was wrong and Caroline was wrong to give in to her bullying. I wouldn't have.' I told her she was stirring. She responded: 'I would hope that I am stirring against your frankly disgraceful attitude and I am not lying. You are bullying, trying to silence.'[2]

For the crime of daring to suggest that racism is still a problem in Britain, I had been smeared by a former Member of Parliament. Simply using my voice was tantamount to being a bullying disgrace. Old racist stereotypes were being resurrected, and I found myself on the receiving end of them. I was a social problem, a disruptive force, a tragic example of a problem community.

Years later, while writing this book, I contacted Caroline Criado-Perez in the hope of getting her perspective on the *Woman's Hour* debacle. She didn't want to speak to me about it.

Even though I write about my experiences with so much contempt, feminism was my first love. It was what gave me a framework to begin understanding the world. My feminist thinking gave rise to my anti-racist thinking, serving as a tool that helped me forge a sense of self-worth. Finding it aged nineteen was perfect timing, equipping me with the skills to navigate adulthood, stand up for myself and work out my own values.

I found feminism a few years before the Twitter and Tumblr generation really took off. It happened in a rather old-fashioned way. As an English literature student, I'd been assigned a stack of books to read for a module on critical theory, which led me to Simone de Beauvoir's *The Second Sex*. As unlikely a situation as it was, the book spoke to me, and I found myself furiously agreeing with the long-dead French existentialist. When she wrote, 'To be feminine is to show oneself as weak, futile, passive, and docile . . . any self-assertion will take away from her femininity and her seductiveness,' it sounded like she was describing my entire existence.

I couldn't find any people in my immediate vicinity who agreed, though. Criticising the misogyny in Shakespeare's *Taming of the Shrew* in a university seminar drew disapproval from my peers, with the majority of my female classmates concluding that 'that's just how it was at the time'. So I sought out feminism elsewhere, spending my student loan money on travel to feminist conferences and events happening around the country. During those years, I met tons of inspiring and passionate women, some who are still my good friends today. Being at feminist events was a relief; to be in a space where people just *got it* – the shared anger, frustration, the burning will to do something, anything, to change the messed-up world we live in. This passion took me to tiny, draughty church halls in little villages in the north-west of England, huddled in a circle surrounded by women my mum's age, and on trains to London, to huge gatherings packed to the brim with hundreds of women – young and old, some new to the movement and some who'd been engaged in activism longer than I'd been alive.

But something wasn't quite right. Feminism was helping me to become a more critical, confident woman, and in turn, it was helping me come to terms with my blackness – a part of myself that I'd always known was shrouded in stigma. I'd grown up with white friends who had assured me that they 'didn't see me as black', and that I 'wasn't like other black people'. Up until then, I'd understood myself as someone who was 'pretty for a black girl', as someone who 'spoke well for where she came from'. I couldn't quite understand why these distinctions were made, but I had a feeling it was to do with class, education – and latent racism. The feminist circles I'd thrown myself into were almost all white. This whiteness wasn't a problem if you didn't talk about race, but if you did, it would reveal itself as an exclusionary force.

A lot of white women in feminist spaces couldn't understand why women of colour needed or wanted a different place to meet, so they would find ways of subtly undermining the self-determination of those who chose to organise separately. At one feminist gathering, there were paper sign-up sheets for every break-out session, designed to keep tabs on the numbers of people attending each one. On the sheet for black feminists, someone had taken the time to vandalise it with their ignorance, simply writing: 'Why?' At another event, a friend held a break-out session called 'the colour of beauty'. With a big stack of fashion and beauty magazines piled in front of her, it was a pretty simple premise, aimed at deconstructing Eurocentric beauty standards. It was primary-school level, really – 'what are the similarities and differences in these pictures?' As others in my group pointed out the models' slimness, I, the only black person in my group, said, 'They're all white.' 'And they've all got long hair,' added a white women eagerly. Laboriously, I explained, 'Yes, but you can grow out your short hair if you want to. I can't change the colour of my skin to fit this beauty standard.' I'm still not sure if she understood what I was saying.

On and on it went like this, tiptoeing around whiteness in feminist spaces. This wasn't a place to be discussing racism, they insisted. There are other places you can go to for that. But that wasn't a choice I could make. My blackness was as much a part of me as my womanhood, and I couldn't separate them.

In my activist days, I joined a small group, named black feminists, so I could speak my truth in a collective full of like-minded women without fear of social punishment. This was a space solely for women of colour. We met once a month to vent and support each other. It was a space I desperately needed.

Meeting with black feminists every month was not unlike the old-school feminist activist method of consciousness-raising. Consciousness-raising was first used by New York Radical Women in the mid-1960s, who in turn took the tactic from America's civil rights movement. In black feminists, we would talk about whatever was happening in our lives. When we met, we began to learn from each other, and I began to realise that other women were experiencing the same things I was. Together we asked why. We took what we thought were isolated incidents, and linked them into a broader context of race and gender.

I met my friend, writer and teacher Lola Okolosie, in that space. 'I'm not sure if those first meetings people were saying "this is structural racism",' she said when we met to reflect on the purpose of the group. 'I think that out of meeting every month, and all of the things that we did in between, analysis started coming, and we were quick to start using that term.

'I just remember people describing what it was, and then everybody else in the room saying "yes, that's happened to me, isn't it infuriating." People were coming at it from lots of different levels. Some were very academic, and some hadn't read any key feminist texts. People's knowledge was very varied. But we were all kind of describing the same hurts, the same frustrations, and the same anger-inducing moments. That, to me, was just absolutely powerful. That it wasn't seen as moaning, that it wasn't seen as reading too deep into things, it was just like yeah, people get it.'

We discussed why it was so important for us to meet without feminists who were white. 'That gaze does so much to silence you,' Lola said. 'Even if you're really confident and really vocal, there is still a holding back that you have to do. Because as a normal human being, you kind of don't really like confrontation. And there's an element of just speaking the truth of what it means to be a black woman in the UK that it would be ridiculous, as a white person, to not read that as implicating you.'

In black feminists, we used the word intersectionality to talk about the crossover of two distinct discriminations – racism and sexism – that happens to people who are both black and women. For black feminist academic Dr Kimberlé Crenshaw, it was her studies in law that led her to coin the now mainstream term. When we met in London's US Embassy, she told me, 'That work started when I realised that African American women were . . . not recognised as having experienced discrimination that reflected both their race and their gender. The courts would say if you don't experience racism in the same way as a [black] man does, or sexism in the same way as a white woman does, then you haven't been discriminated against. I saw that as a problem of sameness and difference. There were claims of being seen as too different to be accommodated by law. That led to intersectionality, looking at the ways race and gender intersect to create barriers and obstacles to equality.'

This was a word to describe the previously undefined phenomenon, although black feminist activists, scholars and theorists had written and spoken about the very same thing years before Dr Crenshaw gave

156

it a name. In 1851, black abolitionist and women's rights activist Sojourner Truth addressed the Ohio Women's Rights Convention.

She said, 'I think that 'twixt de niggers of de South and the women of de North, all talking about rights, the white men will be in a fix pretty soon. But what's all this here talking about? That man over there say that women needs to be helped into carriages, and lifted over ditches, and to have de best place everywhere. Nobody ever helps me into carriages, or over mud-puddles, or gives me any best place! And ain't I a woman? Look at me! Look at my arm! I have ploughed, and planted, and gathered into barns, and no man could head me! And ain't I a woman? Then they talks 'bout this ting in de head; what this they call it?' ('Intellect,' whispered someone near.) 'That's it, honey. What's that got to do with women's rights or niggers' rights? If my cup won't hold but a pint, and yours holds a quart, wouldn't you be mean not to let me have my little half-measure full?'[3] The speech was published twelve years later in the *National Anti-Slavery Standard.*

A century on in 1984, black feminist, activist and poet Audre Lorde wrote in *Sister Outsider: Essays and Speeches:* 'Women of today are still being called upon to stretch across the gap of male ignorance and to educate men as to our existence and our needs. This is an old and primary tool of all oppressors to keep the oppressed occupied with the master's concerns. Now we hear that it is the task of women of colour to educate white women – in the face of tremendous resistance – as to our existence, our differences, our relative roles in our joint survival. This is a diversion of energies and a tragic repetition of racist patriarchal thought.'

In 1979, in her essay 'Anger in isolation: a Black feminist's search for sisterhood' from the essay collection *But Some of Us are Brave*, Michele Wallace wrote: 'We exist as women who are Black who are feminist, each stranded for the moment, working independently because there is not yet an environment in this society remotely congenial to our struggle – because being on the bottom, we would have to do what no one has done: we would have to fight the world.'

Then bell hooks stepped forward in 1981, writing in *Ain't I a Woman: Black Women and Feminism*: 'The process begins with the individual woman's acceptance that . . . women, without exception, are socialized to be racist, classist and sexist, in varying degrees, and that labelling ourselves feminists does not change the fact that we must consciously work to rid ourselves of the legacy of negative socialization. It is obvious that many women have appropriated feminism to serve their own ends, especially those white women who have been at the forefront of the movement; but rather than resigning myself to this appropriation I choose to reappropriate the term "feminism," to focus on the fact that to be "feminist" in any authentic sense of the term is to want for all people, female and male, liberation from sexist role patterns, domination, and oppression.'

And in a law lecture delivered to London's Birkbeck University in late 2013, Angela Davis expanded on the history of how black women have articulated their experiences over the years. In 1969, she explained, American civil rights activist Frances Beale wrote a pamphlet called *Double Jeopardy: To Be Black and Female*. Later, the Third World Women's Alliance created a newspaper called *Triple Jeopardy*. For them, the struggle was not just against racism and sexism, but imperialism too. Elizabeth Spelman's 1988 book *Inessential Woman* challenged the methods of adding on oppressions a year before Dr Kimberlé Crenshaw coined the term 'intersectionality'.

America, with its grid-like road system, neatly packed full of perfect rectangles and squares, was the right place for the birth of this metaphor. Every person knows of a place where all the roads meet. A place where there's no longer one distinct road, but instead a very particular spot, a space that merges all of the roads leading up to it. Black women, in these theories, were proof that the roads didn't run parallel, but instead crossed over each other frequently. And the aforementioned women writers' work thoroughly illustrates how much richness and depth there is to be found when examining those intersections, instead of denying they exist, or forgetting them altogether. For too long, black women have been the forgotten, and have had to come up with strategies of being remembered. In the analysis of who fell through the cracks in competing struggles for rights for women and rights for black people, it always seemed to be *black women* who took the hit.

When black feminists started to push for an intersectional analysis in British feminism, the widespread response from feminists who were white was not one of support. Instead, they began to make the case that the word 'intersectional' was utter jargon – too difficult for anyone without a degree to understand – and therefore useless.

'If you haven't got the same background in or affinity with academia, though, intersectionality is a word that says *this is not for you*,' wrote Sarah Ditum on her personal blog in 2012.[4]

In the *New Statesman*, Holly Baxter and Rhiannon Lucy Cosslett wrote: 'This means that issues of race, class, religion, sexuality, politics and privilege often end up fracturing feminist dialogue, most regularly causing disagreements between those armed with an MA in Gender Studies and a large vocabulary to match, and those without [. . .] Going into certain state comps and discussing the nuances of intersectionality isn't going to have much dice if some of the teenage girls in the audience are pregnant, or hungry, or at risk of abuse (what are they going to do? Protect or feed themselves with theory? Women cannot dine on Greer alone). [. . .] It almost seems as though some educated women want to keep feminism for themselves, cloak it in esoteric theory and hide it under their mattresses, safe and warm beneath the duckdown duvet.'⁵

As the debate intensified on social media, feminists who didn't comply with this line were routinely monstered in the press. The jabs were kept just about evasive enough so that no particular woman was named, and so there was very little response published from those being criticised. Sadie Smith wrote in the *New Statesman*: 'The Online Wimmin Mob takes offence everywhere, but particularly at other women who are not in their little Mean Girls club, which has their own over-stylised and impenetrable language, rules and disciplinary proceedings.'⁶

The white feminist distaste for intersectionality quickly evolved into a hatred of the idea of white privilege – perhaps because to recognise structural racism would have to mean recognising their

WHY I'M NO LONGER TALKING TO

own whiteness. They were backed up by their men. Tom Midlane wrote in the *New Statesman*: 'While the idea is obviously born out of honourable intentions, I believe the whole discourse around privilege is inherently destructive – at best, a colossal distraction, and at worst a means of turning us all into self-appointed moral guardians out to aggressively police even fellow travellers' speech and behaviour. Why does this matter, you ask? The answer is simple: it matters because privilege-checking has thoroughly infected progressive thought.'[7]

You'll notice a trend here. Between 2012 and 2014, the most spirited takedowns of black women talking about race, racism and intersectionality were always published via the *New Statesman*, Britain's foremost centre-left political magazine. Because of the sheer frequency of these takedowns, I began to wonder if there was an editorial line. There were weak efforts by the *New Statesman* to publish rebuttals by defenders of intersectionality, but it was the harsh criticisms that seemed to set the magazine's agenda on the topic.

A few years later, the arguments first put forward by white feminists and left-wing bloggers in 2012 and 2013 were being echoed by publishing platforms that were decidedly *not* left wing. The extreme, hard-right, website *Breitbart London* defined intersectionality as 'A debate strategy: when you're losing an argument about feminism, call your opponent racist or, even more damningly, capitalist', and defined privilege as 'What white middle-class feminists have and their victims don't'.[8] In another dictionary-style takedown of progressives, the *Spectator* wrote: 'I is for identity politics. Always define yourself by your natural characteristics rather than your character, achievements or beliefs. You are first and foremost male, female, other, straight, gay, black or white and should refer to yourself as such. Martin Luther King should have checked his privilege when he had that nonsense dream of a world where people "will not be judged by the colour of their skin, but by the content of their character". That's easy for a middle-class straight man to say, Marty. I is also for intersectionality, the tearaway offspring of identity politics, where you must constantly wonder how your various personal identities intersect with each other (or something).'[9] On the same topic, another writer in the same magazine wrote, 'As theories go, this one isn't wholly mad. The trouble is, it has become faddish among people who don't read books or essays but merely tweets and Internet comments, and thus don't know what they are talking about. So what you end up with is a kind of minority Top Trumps, and a sort of spreading, infectious belief that the more box-tickingly disadvantaged a person is, the wiser, kinder and more all-seeing they must be. And it's stupid.'[10]

Based on these responses, it seemed like black women's interventions in white British feminism were absolutely not welcome. The reaction was identical to the way the most sexist of men treat feminism. In the middle of this heated debate about intersectionality in British feminism, four months after my disastrous conversation with BBC *Woman's Hour*, Dr Kimberlé Crenshaw was invited onto the same show to explain why feminism can no longer ignore race. She was asked 'how helpful is it when . . . black women are asking white and well-off women to check their privilege?' Quoting some of black feminism's harshest critics, the interviewer continued, 'It's closing down the debate, and it's diminishing empathy.'

'That's always going to be an issue in any kind of movement that makes a claim that everybody in the category is experiencing discrimination in the same way, when in fact, that's not often the case,' Dr Crenshaw responded. But the damage was done. The utterance of a meme-ified phrase saw black feminism reduced to nothing more than a disruptive force, upsetting sweet, polite, palatable white feminism. British feminism was characterised as a movement where everything was peaceful until the angry black people turned up. The white feminist's characterisations of black feminists as disruptive aggressors was not so different from broader stereotyping of black communities by the press. Women of colour were positioned as the immigrants of feminism, unwelcome but tolerated – a reluctantly dealt-with social problem. It's surprising that no prominent white feminists made it far enough in their hyperbole to give an Enoch Powell-style, impassioned speech – something along the lines of 'in this country in fifteen or twenty years' time the black woman will have the whip hand over the white woman'. Considering the verbal violence with which they greeted a race analysis in feminism, this seemed to be the logical conclusion of their arguments.

It's important to see the white feminist push-back against intersectionality not in isolation, but rather in the historical context of establishment clampdowns on the black struggle. All the signs were there: a closing of ranks, paired with a campaign of misinformation, lies and discrediting. When Louise Mensch wrote her aggressive tweets about me, the women she felt she was supporting were doyennes of the left – regular writers for left-leaning publications like the *Guardian* and the *New Statesman*. They were supported by white, well-known writers and figures of a host of different political persuasions. But at that point, their minor political differences didn't matter. The white consensus in feminism required defending, and they needed to club together to do it. My speaking up about racism in feminism, to them, was akin to a violent attack on their very idea of themselves.

This is how racism perpetuates itself in all spaces, feminist or otherwise. My situation was very public. But back then I had a feeling that similar scenarios were playing out across the country – in workplaces, in social circles, in families; and the result everywhere was a person of colour with no support network, doubting themselves.

In British feminism, questioning whether a woman could have feminist politics and do traditionally feminine things was a sentiment that intrigued women's magazines in the 1990s and early 2000s. Can you be a feminist and wear high heels, the magazines asked. Can you be a feminist and wear make-up? Can you be a feminist and get your nails done? These were the most facile of questions, giving rise to the most facile of magazine features. The 'can you be a feminist and' questions were all predicated on tired stereotypes of feminist activism from the 1970s patriarchal press, depicting feminists as dungaree-wearing angry women who sought to crush men under their Dr Marten-clad feet. In this stereotype of the scary imaginary feminist that no woman would ever want to be, her appearance was the antithesis of all beauty standards.

It was complete rubbish, of course. If the last five years have taught us anything, it's that feminism is a broad church that has less to do with the upkeep of your appearance, and more to do with the upkeep of your politics. Instead of asking about high heels and lipstick, the pressing questions we have always needed to ask are: Can you be a feminist and be anti-choice? Can you be a feminist and be wilfully ignorant on racism?

Feminist themes seem to be ever-present in television and film at the moment. This is a marked improvement from the media that went before it. Feminism is thriving in journalism and music, and it is all over social media with no signs of subsiding. The people who are calling themselves feminists are getting younger and younger, due in part to their favourite pop stars and actresses demystifying the word. Each time a celebrity stakes her claim on feminism, a little bit of the stigma surrounding the word is shattered.

With countrywide political landmarks like the legalisation of same-sex marriage, everyone is keen to look like they approve of progress. But among feminists, there are a few ideological standpoints – race, reproductive rights, conservatism – that continue to cause immovable fault lines in the movement. Too often, a white feminist's ideological standpoint does not see racism as a problem, let alone a priority. The backlash against intersectionality was white feminism in action.

When the phrase 'white feminism', used as a derogatory term, picked up circulation in the feminist lexicon, its popularity made some feminists who are white somewhat agitated. But this knee-jerk backlash against the phrase – to what is more often than not a rigorous critique of the consequences of structural racism – was undoubtedly born from an entitled need to defend whiteness rather than any yearning to reflect on the meaning of the phrase 'white feminism'. What does it mean for your feminist politics to be strangled, stoppered, and hindered by whiteness?

If feminism can understand the patriarchy, it's important to question why so many feminists struggle to understand whiteness as a political structure in the very same way. Similar to the fact that they are man-heavy, our most recognised political structures are white-dominated. In that space of overwhelming whiteness, there is always a wide range of opinions to be found. So much of politics is just middle-aged white men passing the ball to one another. Every so often, a white middle-aged woman is brought on board in an effort to diversify. The one thing that unites these differing political perspectives is their flat-out refusal to challenge a white consensus.

White feminism is a politics that engages itself with myths such as 'I don't see race'. It is a politics which insists that talking about race fuels racism – thereby denying people of colour the words to articulate our existence. It's a politics that expects people of colour to quietly assimilate into institutionally racist structures without kicking up a fuss. It's a politics where people of colour are never setting the agenda. Instead, they are relegated to constantly reacting to things and frantically playing catch-up. A white-dominated feminist political consensus allows people of colour a place at the table if we're willing to settle for tokenism, but it clamps down if they attempt to create accountability for said consensus – let alone any structural change.

Whiteness positions itself as the norm. It refuses to recognise itself for what it is. Its so-called 'objectivity' and 'reason' is its most potent and insidious tool for maintaining power. White feminism can be conceptualised as the feminist wing of said political consensus. It's a set of white-centred feminist values and beliefs that some women like to buy into. Other factors, like class indicators, play a huge part in it.

White feminism in itself isn't particularly threatening. It becomes a problem when its ideas dominate – presented as the universal, to be applied to all women. It is a problem, because we consider humanity through the prism of whiteness. It is inevitable that feminism wouldn't be immune from this. Consequently, white feminism enforces its position when those who challenge it are considered troublemakers. When I write about white feminism, I'm not reducing white women to the colour of their skin. Whiteness is a political position, and challenging it in feminist spaces is not a tit-for-tat disagreement because prejudice needs power to be effective.

The politics of whiteness transcends the colour of anyone's skin. It is an occupying force in the mind. It is a political ideology that is concerned with maintaining power through domination and exclusion. Anyone can buy into it, just like anyone can choose to challenge it. White women seem to take the phrase 'white feminism' very personally, but it is at once everything and nothing to do with them. It's not about women, who are feminists, who are white. It's about women espousing feminist politics as they buy into the politics of whiteness, which at its core are exclusionary, discriminatory and structurally racist.

For those who identify as feminist, but have never questioned what it means to be white, it is likely the phrase white feminism applies. Those who perceive every critique of white-dominated politics to be an attack on them as a white person are probably part of the problem. When white feminists are ignorant on race, they don't initially come from a place of malice – although their opposition can very quickly evolve into a frothing vitriol when challenged on their politics. Instead, I've learnt that they come from a place very similar to mine. We all grew up in a white-dominated world. This is the context that white feminists are working within, benefiting from and reproducing a system that they barely notice. However, their critical-analysis skills are pretty good at spotting exclusive systems, such as gender, that they *don't* benefit from. They spout impassioned rhetoric against patriarchy with ease, feeling its sharp edge of injustice jutting them in the ribs at work in the form of unequal pay, and socially, hurled at them in the street in the form of catcalling. And they rightly say, 'I'm sick of living in this world built for the needs of men! I feel like at best, I can fight it, at worst I have to learn to cope in it.' Yet they're incredibly defensive when the same analysis of race is levelled at their whiteness. You'd have to laugh, if the whole thing wasn't so reprehensible.

When they talk about equal rights and representation, white feminists deeply mean it. They can be witty, intelligent, eloquent and insightful on issues like reproductive rights, street harassment, sexual violence, beauty standards, body image, and women's representation in the media. These are issues that so many women can strongly resonate with and relate to. It tends to be white women who find themselves representing feminism in the press, talking about it on television or the radio, enthusing about it in magazines.

It helps that the white women espousing feminist politics in the public sphere are conventionally attractive with enough of a quirk that renders them relatable to the everyday woman. They have chubby thighs or gappy teeth. They have bodies that are far from the supermodel standard that we've come to hold all women in the public eye to. This is refreshing, we shout. These women look like us. These women are real. These women are women's women. These women are not afraid to say what they think. In an age of Twitter followings and YouTube subscriber counts, it's also about personal branding and burgeoning careers. So we click, and like, and follow.

Being a feminist with a race analysis means seeing clearly how race and gender are intertwined when it comes to inequalities. Looking at the politics of race in this country, I can see how an entitlement towards white British women's bodies plays out in what is being said. 2066 is the year white people will suppos- edly become a minority in Britain. Oxford Professor David Coleman is the man who estimated that date. In 2016, he wrote in a *Daily Mail* article – framed around the issue of Brexit: 'women born overseas contributed 27 per cent of all live births in 2014, and 33 per cent of births had at least one immi- grant parent – a figure which has more than doubled since the 1990s.'[11] The article was titled, 'RIP This Britain: With academic objectivity, Oxford Professor and population expert David Coleman says white Britons could be in the minority by the 2060s – or sooner'.

I think it's easy to see how those who espouse white nationalist politics could take these figures and run with them, and insist that the year 2066 will mark Britain's doomsday. It looks like there is a subtle ethno-nationalism in this discussion, almost worthy of *The Handmaid's Tale*. It seems to be a racialised misogyny that is preoccupied with wombs, and urges white British women to fuck for their country while accusing women who aren't white British of breeding uncontrollably and destabilising the essence of Britain.

Despite this pernicious narrative, there are quarters of British society who maintain that misogyny is somehow the reserve of foreigners. Never in a million years did I think I'd hear former Prime Minister David Cameron call out the ills of a patriarchal society. When, in 2012 and 2013, British women's groups such as the Fawcett Society and the Women's Budget Group did the laborious maths to argue that the government's austerity agenda was hitting women the hardest, David Cameron and his party barely responded. It was interesting, then, that when Mr Cameron finally uttered the words 'patriarchal society' almost three years later, it was to lay out government plans of an ultimatum policy that demanded Muslim women who were living in the UK on a spousal visa either learn English, or face deportation.

'Look, I'm not blaming the people who can't speak English,' he told BBC Radio 4's *Today* programme. 'Some of these people have come to our country [from] quite sort of patriarchal societies, where perhaps the menfolk haven't wanted them to learn English, haven't wanted them to integrate.' He continued, 'What we've found in some of the work we've done is . . . [a] school governors' meeting where the men sit in the meeting and the women have to sit outside, [and] women who aren't allowed to leave their home without a male relative. This is happening in our country and it's not acceptable. We should be very proud of our values, our liberalism, our tolerance, our idea that we want to build a genuine opportunity democracy . . . where there is segregation it's holding people back, it's not in tune with British values and it needs to go.'[12]

Speaking on national radio, Cameron let it be known that alongside dedicated funding for Muslim women in what he called 'isolated communities' to learn English, the plans would also come with compulsory language tests for these women within two and a half years of them arriving in Britain. As surreal as it was to hear David Cameron challenging a patriarchal society, it wasn't surprising that his idea of patriarchy was described in direct opposition to our own advanced, so-called egalitarian and meritocratic British sense of self.

When we tell ourselves that misogyny is simply an import from overseas, we are saying that it's just not a problem here. David Cameron probably shouldn't be too quick to insinuate that extreme misogyny is a foreign import to the British Isles. When the Office of National Statistics shows that, on average, seven women a month in England and Wales are murdered by a current or former partner,[13] and 85,000 women are raped in England and Wales alone every year,[14] we know that this is simply not the case. Misogyny is not a problem that can be solved with closed borders, nor a crash course in Received Pronunciation. It exists in the psyche of what it means to be a man in every country.

Despite this truth, it was the idea that multiculturalism brings with it a corrosive sexism and misogyny that was touted after mass sexual assaults took place on New Year's Eve of 2015 in Cologne, Germany. The same angle emerged when a child sexual exploitation ring run by Asian men was uncovered in Rotherham, south Yorkshire, in 2013. In 2012 and 2013, the phrase 'Asian sex gang' occupied what seemed like a million headlines. The far right loves this Asian sex-gang angle. To them, the women are their property, the women are 'ours'. But the reality is that if every Asian man left the country, child sexual exploitation on British Isles would not go away.

There is a race aspect to these incidents that can't be ignored, and acknowledging this doesn't invalidate any condemnation of grooming, abuse and misogyny. A lot of the time, being a black feminist situates you between a rock and a hard place, challenging the racism you see targeted at black and brown people and also challenging the patriarchy around you. And while the endless tug of war of political debate demands clear rights and wrongs, this topic desperately requires nuance.

What is undeniable is that Western beauty ideals and Western objectification of female flesh focuses heavily on whiteness and on youth. White female flesh is commoditised in the public eye all the time. If black and brown flesh is ever included in these forums, it's often considered a novelty – perhaps described as 'ebony', 'chocolate' or 'caramel', sometimes approached as taboo. Amid the No More Page 3 campaign was the little-referenced point that black Page 3 girls rarely exist, presumably because some media didn't believe that black and brown women are beautiful enough to bother objectifying. There are, of course, exceptions to this rule, often in entertainment and media in which creative control is designed to pander to the needs of black and brown men.

Let's look at how racialised bodies sit inside an understanding of sex and sexual abuse in a world drunk on overwhelming whiteness. Racist beauty ideals encourage a culture of certain types of female flesh being considered publicly available. After two Pakistani men were jailed in 2011 for raping and sexually abusing young white girls, it seemed like Jack Straw, former MP for Blackburn, took on the language of the abuser when he said that white girls were seen as 'easy meat' for Asian rapists. Speaking on BBC *Newsnight*, he said, 'These young men are in a Western society, in any event, they act like any other young men, they're fizzing and popping with testosterone, they want some outlet for that, but Pakistani heritage girls are off-limits and they are expected to marry a Pakistani girl from Pakistan, typically.'[15] There was pushback on his comments from other politicians, but the objections started and ended with indignation that Straw was stereotyping an entire community.

What was missed was how Jack Straw not only echoed abusers, but also failed to challenge their language. First he indulged in the 'boys will be boys' excuse, as though fizzing and popping with testosterone is a precursor to violating another human being's body. It never is, yet this pervasive belief excuses abuse and coercion as simply youthful curiosity. His second error was fairly simple: women are not flesh to be consumed. Women aren't objects, passive and docile and open and waiting. There is something so insidious about this language of food and flesh, one that suggests that men must eat as much meat and fuck as many women as possible in order to be the manliest. In our gender relations, 'meat' strips women of basic bodily autonomy, asserting that we are only ever on the menu, and never at the table.

This, plus a feeling of public piety around the hijab, the niqab, and covered black and brown female flesh in particular, makes for a toxic combination. The modesty expectation is just as limiting and judgemental as the compulsory bikini-body one. Both obsessively focus on a woman's looks and how covered or uncovered her body is in determining her value, as though her body belongs to a male gaze before it belongs to her. There are always external factors influencing the way a women dresses, but the ultimate decision should be her own. All the while, in the case of the aforementioned abuses, the voices of poor white women and girls; and the voices of black and brown women and girls are denied any agency. This is not simply a question of patriarchy; it's a manifestation of the virgin/whore dichotomy that spans across postcodes, countries and cultures.

We cannot effectively destroy this kind of exploitation without attacking pervasive cultural messages, at home and away, that tell men that women's bodies are always up for the taking. As long as women are groped on public transport, masturbated at in the street, and as long as female flesh stares dead-eyed and pouty-lipped from millions of images advertising goods as banal as exercise supplements and hooded jackets, we will have a misogyny problem.

As we challenge racist, Islamophobic stories regarding sexual abuse, we've also got to challenge patriarchy where we find it. One cannot be done effectively without the other. At present, the conversation about misogyny that has reached the highest levels of government has maintained that it is a foreign import. This is disingenuous and it is done to pull the wool over our eyes. Feminist activists would be foolish to ally with political forces that only ever speak in defence of women when there are Muslims to bash.

So, we know that as much as the subject needs nuance, groups of white men who rape and abuse children and babies are reported on by the press, but their crimes are not seized upon as indicative of the inherent problem with *men* in the same way that men of colour's crimes are held up as evidence of the savagery of their race. When an organised gang of seven white men were found guilty of raping and abusing children (or conspiring to) in April 2015, the far right did not co-opt the story as evidence that we should deport all men from the country. The seven men, who were scattered across the UK, communicated online and streamed abuse to each other using conference-call technology. All the while, they were embedding themselves in their separate communities and grooming the parents of the children they were preying on. One even befriended a pregnant woman with a view to abusing her unborn baby. According to the BBC's reporting on the cases, officers from the National Crime Agency called the crimes the most 'vile and depraved' they'd ever seen. These white men's crimes didn't get an affix of their race in the consequent headlines.

We as a nation hate paedophiles. We malign them because they are paedophiles. But crucially, we see them as anomalies. We don't think that their actions are because of the deviancy of white men. When white men target babies, children and teenagers for sexual gratification, we don't ask for a deep reflection on these actions from the white male community.

This isn't about good men or bad men – binary notions that we feel comfortable enough with to slot into neat boxes – but about rape culture. We should be asking why, when children and women speak up about being raped or sexually assaulted, there are always people around them who bend over back-wards to try and find ways to suggest that she incited or invited it. We should question the class prejudice that allowed white, poor victims to be ignored by the authorities in a way that would be less likely to hap-pen to a middle-class white girl raised in Islington. Class assigns your life with a correspondent value in the eyes of gatekeepers. The taboo in discussing these crimes isn't about race, it is about men. Predatory men. Every woman who has ever been a teenage girl could tell you a tale about an encounter with a predatory man, men who smell youth and vulnerability, and seek only to dominate.

Far from shutting down debate, incorporating the challenges of racism is absolutely essential for a feminist movement that doesn't leave anyone behind. I'm not sure our most popular versions of feminism are currently up to that task.

I fear that, although white feminism is palatable to those in power, when it has won, things will look very much the same. Injustice will thrive, but there will be more women in charge of it. Feminism is not about equality, and certainly not about silently slipping into a world of work created by and for men. Feminism, at its best, is a movement that works to liberate all people who have been economically, socially and culturally marginalised by an ideological system that has been designed for them to fail. That means disabled people, black people, trans people, women and non-binary people, LGB people and working-class people. The idea of campaigning for equality must be complicated if we are to untangle the situation we're in. Feminism will have won when we have ended poverty. It will have won when women are no longer expected to work two jobs (the care and emotional labour for their families as well as their day jobs) by default.

The mess we are living is a deliberate one. If it was created by people, it can be dismantled by people, and it can be rebuilt in a way that serves all, rather than a selfish, hoarding few. Beyond the obvious demands – an end to sexual violence, an end to the wage gap – feminism must be class-conscious, and aware of the limiting culture of the gender binary. It needs to recognise that disabled people aren't inherently defective, but rather that non-disabled people have failed at creating a physical world that serves all. Feminism must demand affordable, decent, secure housing, and a universal basic income. It should demand pay for full-time mothers and free childcare for working mothers. It should recognise that we live in a world in which women are constantly harangued into being lusted after, but punishes sex workers for using that situation to make a living. Feminism needs to thoroughly recognise that sexuality is fluid, and we need to dream of a world where people are not violently policed for transgressing rigid gender roles. Feminism needs to demand a world in which racist history is acknowledged and accounted for, in which reparations are distributed, in which race is completely deconstructed.

I understand that these demands are utopian and unrealistic. But I think feminism *has* to be absolutely utopian and unrealistic, far removed from any semblance of the world we're living in now. We have to hope for and envision something before agitating for it, rather than blithely giving up, citing reality, and accepting the way things are. After all, utopian ideals are as ideological as the political foundations of the world we're currently living in. Above everything, feminism is a constant work in progress. We are all still learning.

I have always loved feminism's readiness to viciously rip into the flesh of misogyny, to stick its chin out defiantly and scare the living daylights out of mediocre men. But it needs to be the whole package, to take into account every aspect of what writer bell hooks called 'the white supremacist capitalist patriarchy'. Feminism doesn't work well as a polite, gender-only analysis that is neat and unchallenging enough to be accepted in corporate environments. It has failed when it works as an unwittingly exclusive movement that isn't self-aware enough to recognise where its participants benefit from the current system. At the point in which feminism has become a placidly white movement that claims to work on behalf of all women, but doesn't question its own overwhelming whiteness, we really need to think about starting again.

Demands for equality need to be as complicated as the inequalities they attempt to address. The question is: who do we want to be equal to? Men, like women, are not homogeneous. The Chancellor of the

Exchequer leads a very different life to the postman who pushes letters through my front door every day. He has had access to vastly different opportunities in his life than his governmental counterpart. He probably wasn't born into wealth, and his parents probably couldn't stump up the cash to get him into an elite private school that would buy him upper-class entitlement for the rest of his life. Men inhabit different spaces. Some face racism. Some face homophobia. Even if we as feminists decide to put the differences between men aside, does equality demand parity with people who have always had a disproportionately large share of resources?

It's clear that equality doesn't quite cut it. Asking for a sliver of disproportional power is too polite a request. I don't want to be included. Instead, I want to question who created the standard in the first place. After a lifetime of embodying difference, I have no desire to be equal. I want to deconstruct the structural power of a system that marked me out as different. I don't wish to be assimilated into the status quo. I want to be liberated from all negative assumptions that my characteristics bring. The onus is not on *me* to change. Instead, it's the world around me.

Equality is fine as a transitional demand, but it's dishonest not to recognise it for what it is – the easy route. There is a difference between saying 'we want to be included' and saying 'we want to reconstruct your exclusive system'. The former is more readily accepted into the mainstream.

There is such stigma attached to speaking up and being a woman, let alone speaking up, being a woman, and being black. When, in 2013, model Naomi Campbell lent her voice to a campaign dedicated to getting more models of colour on the runways of Fashion Week (the statistic at the time was that 82 per cent of Fashion Week models were white), she was confronted by a Channel 4 News reporter who told her 'you have a reputation, rightly or wrongly, for being quite an angry person.'[16]

The angry black woman cannot be reasoned with. She argues back. She is not docile, sweet or agreeable, like expectations of white femininity. Her anger makes her ugly and undesirable. It's for that reason she'll never find a husband, and if she does, she will emasculate him. Emasculation as a concept is one that requires the rigid upholding of sexist gender roles. The angry black woman stereotype wields misogyny as a stick to beat black women over the head with. That angry black women appear to emasculate men is sexist because it makes assumptions about the characteristics of men that inevitably limits the scope of their humanity. To believe in emasculation, you have to believe that masculinity is about power, and strength, and dominance. These traits are supposed to be great in men, but they're very unattractive in women. Especially angry black ones. Women in general aren't supposed to be angry. Women are expected to smile, swallow our feelings and be self-sacrificial. Bossy is ugly, and of course, the worst thing a woman could ever be is ugly. As black women, our blackness already situates us further along the ugliness scale. God forbid we be fat.

The 'angry black woman' phrase says more about maleness and whiteness than it does about black women. It speaks to a status quo that recognises its own simultaneous suffocating dominance and delicate fragility – of the reality of its increasing irrelevance over time, and a compulsive need to stop that looming change.

I used to be scared of being perceived as an angry black woman. But I soon realised that any number of authentic emotions I displayed could and would be interpreted as anger. My assertiveness, passion and excitement could all be wielded against me. Not displaying anger wasn't going to stop me being labelled as angry, so I thought: fuck it. I decided to speak my mind. The more politically assertive I became, the more men shouted at me. Performance artist Selina Thompson told me that when she thinks of what it means to be an angry black woman, she thinks of honesty. There is no point in keeping quiet because you want to be liked. Often, there will be no one fighting your corner but yourself. It was black feminist poet Audre Lorde who said: 'your silence will not protect you.' Who wins when we don't speak? Not us.

6

RACE AND CLASS

In the time that I've spent writing and publicly speaking about race, I've become familiar with one particular question. 'What about class?' It's a question that follows me everywhere I go. In it is an implication that it's class, not race, that is the true battle to be fought in Britain – and that we have to choose between one or the other. I totally reject this assumption. But I'm going to try and answer the question. What *about* class? And how does it relate to race – if it does at all?

In Britain, class is integral to how we understand our own position in society. Since the Victorian times, we have confined ourselves to one of three categories – working class, middle class, or upper class. We've understood class in a Marxist fashion, using a person's relationship to the means of production as a defining factor. The saying goes that if you're paid by the hour and you rent your home, then you're working class, and if you're paid monthly and you own your home, you're middle class. But we no longer have a country full of factories, mines and mills with rigid structures of workers and bosses. I grew up in a generation defined by watching people older than me benefit from seemingly endless credit, so the demarcation between rich and poor was hard to spot. By the time I was twelve, the then Prime Minister Tony Blair announced that he wanted to see 50 per cent of young adults in higher education by the year 2010. Going to university was no longer a clear indication of class. In my generation, your first job was likely to be on a shop floor, in catering, or in a call centre. The language of blue-collar and white-collar workers never really resonated. Post-2008 recession, these categories have become even more blurred as job security for most became a dream rather than a reality.

Because we are a nation that loves to think of itself as the underdog, it wasn't surprising that a 2016 British Social Attitudes survey found that 60 per cent of the British public identifies as working class. The most interesting part of the survey was that 47 per cent of those who considered themselves working class were actually in managerial and professional jobs – hardly working class at all. In its analysis of the numbers, the survey called this identification the 'working class of the mind'. And although there was no breakdown of survey respondents by racial demographics, those who identified as working class but were in middle-class jobs were more likely to have anti-immigrant politics.[1] When people ask me 'what about class?' when I talk about race, I can't help but wonder if they're not really talking about money, but instead a particular mindset.

One of the most successful and vigorous studies on class in recent years was the Great British Class Survey, commissioned by the BBC. Around 160,000 people took part. The results, published in 2013, revealed there were not just three classes, but seven. The elite are the wealthiest people in the country, scoring highest economically, socially and culturally. The established middle class are the next wealthiest. They love culture. They're followed by the technical middle class, who have money, but are not very social. New affluent workers score middle-wise on income but high on socialising and culture. They're coming from working-class backgrounds, and are less likely to have gone to university. The traditional working class are, on average, the oldest group. Emergent service workers lag behind them in terms of financial security. Lastly, there's the precariat – the most deprived group.[2]

Unlike many other class surveys, the BBC's collected information on the race of its participants. You'll find most people of colour in the emergent service workers' group, making up 21 per cent of it. We're also over twice as likely to be found in the emergent service workers' group than in the traditional working-class group. And materially, we are actually poorer.

I say 'we', because according to the calculator, I am an emergent service worker, along with 19 per cent of the population. We tend to be young, and we live in urban areas. A lot of us aren't white. We have high cultural and social capital, but barely any economic capital. Our income averages at around £21,000. That's higher than the traditional working class, who tend to be living in post-industrial areas of England. They are much more likely to own their own home, and have more money in savings than my group. The Great British Class Survey report concluded that emergent service workers – arts and humanities graduates doing bar work, or working in call centres – are the children of the traditional working class. My guess is that they're also the children of immigrants.

This information suggests that it's not as simple or binary as choosing between race and class when thinking about structural inequalities. Not only does the three-tiered class hierarchy no longer really exist, but it looks like existing race inequalities are compounded rather than erased by class inequalities. In the wake of the 2015 summer budget, analysis from race equality think tank the Runnymede Trust found that 4 million black and minority ethnic people would be worse off as a result of it, that BME people were over-represented in areas hit by the budget, and that race inequality will worsen over time because of it. The reality is, if you are born not white in this country, you probably haven't been born into wealth. Research from the Joseph Rowntree Foundation has shown that black and minority ethnic people are much more likely to live in income poverty than their white counterparts. At the time of their research, the foundation found that just 20 per cent of white Brits were living in income poverty, in drastic comparison to 30 per cent of black Caribbeans, 45 per cent of black Africans, 55 per cent of Pakistanis and 65 per cent of Bangladeshis. The report also found that a disturbing 50 per cent of black and minority ethnic children were living in poverty.[3]

But that Joseph Rowntree report was published in 2007. Looking at census data provides a more long-term analysis of race and poverty in Britain. Published in 2014, analysis from the 2011 census focused on race and the labour market found that black men aged between 16 to 64 have the highest unemployment rates in the country, and that black women are more likely to be unemployed than white women. When it comes to the type of work that people in Britain are doing, the evidence again correlates along race lines. Pakistani, black African and Bangladeshi men are the most likely to work in low-skilled (and low-paid) jobs. According to the census, low-skilled jobs include admin, care work, sales and customer service, and operating machines. Asian people are concentrated in sectors like accommodation, food and retail, whereas BME women are concentrated in health and social work (meaning that when these public services face government cuts, black women feel it especially hard). Pakistani and Indian men can be found in the wholesale, retail and mechanics sectors.[4] These are not exactly middle-class jobs.

These are the objective figures. They suggest that many consider their class to be about their preferred culture and politics, rather than their relationship to assets and wealth. Unlike race and racism, it is generally accepted in Britain your class can either positively or negatively affect your lot in life. But race is rarely brought into the analysis. Instead, when we think about inequality, we are encouraged to think of both race and class as distinct and separate. They're not.

None of this is to say that white people aren't living in poverty in Britain. Rather, it's to point out that the working-class people in this country are not all white. In the face of an assumption around class that seems to be hung up solely on the purity of British racial exclusivity, we should ask ourselves who exactly makes up the working class.

Never has the conversation about class and inequality felt more urgent than in the recent discussion about London's housing crisis – on the lack of available social housing, on the barely regulated private rental sector, and the increasingly futile pursuit of home ownership. In the capital, the invasion of luxury flats built for people on extraordinarily high incomes appeared to start in the east and quickly began to spread north. Construction was alarmingly swift. I spent half of my childhood in Tottenham, north-east London. When I go back to visit friends and family, I see the area changing. Walking down one Tottenham street on an autumn evening, I noticed that what was once an area of demolition had sprung up into skeletal scaffolding. The grounds were surrounded with boarding, and the boarding was plastered with aspirational images. The words on the boarding were in equal parts sinister as they were inviting.

The reading really depended on who caught a glimpse of it at the time. 'Enjoy a more urban side to living in the heart of north London,' the lettering read. This was an invitation that was not aimed towards people already living in Tottenham, but to newcomers – perhaps first-time buyers desperate to get on the property ladder with help from the bank of Mum and Dad, or maybe buy-to-let landlords whose sole aim was to make money out of London's housing crisis. The word 'urban' here was coded, a term that implied inner cities, poverty and dilapidation. Urban here, as it is so often used (in music particularly), was code language for 'black people live here'. The 2011 census saw 65 per cent of Haringey residents report that they were not white British. I was suspicious of the sudden increase of Tottenham new-builds, worried that they might begin to usher in an era of gentrification – with huge implications for the class and racial make-up of the area.

My suspicions weren't unfounded. In 2013, *The Economist* reported that in the neighbouring London borough of Hackney between the years 2001 and 2011, Stoke Newington's white British population jumped by 15 per cent and Dalston's by 26 per cent.[5] Fuelled by gentrification, the change wasn't just about race, but about wealth, affluence and mobility. It was also about class.

After noticing the first 'urban living' invitation, I saw similar new-build construction sites popping up all over Tottenham. In 2015, barriers around the freshly built Rivers Apartments on the Spurs end of Tottenham High Road promised passers-by a 'major sport-led development for Tottenham' – new homes, a new school and new jobs. Fascinated by the race and class implications of London's housing boom, I decided to look into it – and began rifling through the council's publicly available documents.

The same year, Haringey Council planned to build 1,900 homes in Tottenham by 2018. This was promised to be part of a £131 million regeneration programme, with funding secured from the city's most senior administrative body, the Greater London Authority. On the face of it, this seemed like a positive contribution to meeting the high level of demand for housing in the borough of Haringey. In mid-2015, its housing waiting list had over 4,500 people looking for somewhere to live. The council decided that half the homes built would be affordable, two-thirds of which would be affordable rent, and one-third would be shared ownership. As a response to the housing crisis, it couldn't have been more timely.

But when I looked deeper into the borough's regeneration plans, I found a different picture. An intriguing coalition of people had aligned to question exactly who the new housing in Tottenham would benefit, and they made convincing claims about race, class, wealth and access. One activist told me: 'We're not opposed to regeneration. This is a community and an area that needs regeneration and investment for the existing residents.' His view was echoed by another housing activist, who said: 'People would like to see improvements. But what kind of improvements, and who for?'

The question was whether low-income local residents in most need – who were mostly black – would benefit from the new housing at all. The crux of criticism against Haringey's housing plans surrounded the council's decision to 'place a high priority on affordable home ownership'. The council's own equality impact assessment (EQIA) of its housing strategy read: 'There is a possibility that, over time, black residents in Haringey may not benefit from the plans to build more homes in the borough through promoting affordable home ownership in east Haringey. White households may benefit more easily.' The 250 homes available at affordable social rent that Haringey planned to build by the year 2018 accounted for just 5 per cent of the number of people waiting to be homed, the EQIA concluded. It was damning. But at the time, Haringey Council argued that they needed to sell some homes privately because the funding available from central government wasn't enough for the whole project.

To truly understand what happened here, you need to think about these housing plans in the context of Tottenham's history of race and class. In 2015 the average Haringey resident earned around £24,000 a year. That figure is above the national average of £22,044, but below the inner-London average salary of £34,473. However, Haringey's average earnings were skewed by the vast income inequalities in the borough.

The council calls this the 'east–west divide'. In east Haringey's Tottenham Hale, where the new housing was proposed, the highest amount of residents work in jobs like sales and services, cleaning, delivering goods, collecting the bins. That's in comparison to 23.9 per cent of Haringey's overall residents working in professional occupations. This is a clear class divide. Home ownership is high in the affluent west of the borough – areas like Muswell Hill, Crouch

End and Highgate – while residents in the east of the borough – areas like Seven Sisters, White Hart Lane and Tottenham Hale – live mostly in social housing. Similarly, high salaries can be found in west Haringey, while low pay is found in east Haringey. These fault lines are compounded by race, with white people disproportionately represented in the west of the borough, and black people disproportionately represented in the east. In the west Haringey wards of Muswell Hill, Crouch End and Highgate, more than 80 per cent of residents are white, in comparison to around 40 per cent of residents in the east Haringey wards of Northumberland Park and Tottenham Hale.

A report from the Runnymede Trust and Manchester University declared Haringey one of the most unequal places in England and Wales.[6] And according to the council's equalities impact assessment on its own housing strategy, it is single mothers in the borough who are most likely to be homeless. The numbers of single mothers registering as homeless in 2015 was increasing. It was fair to conclude that it was women – almost certainly the majority black, almost certainly mothers – who were being pushed into precarious living situations. Their council responded by ignoring their needs in its housing plans.

In March of 2015, dissent at the council's regeneration plans had spilled over into local government. The general committee of Tottenham Constituency Labour

Party, an organisation of local party members, unanimously passed an emergency resolution noting its concern that the council's housing plans had 'placed the onus on black residents to increase their income to be able to afford the new homes on offer, and not required or considered what the council should be doing to enable equality of opportunity and eliminate discrimination'. The resolution wasn't the policy of Tottenham CLP's councillors, but it did an effective job of displaying the general feeling of discontent.

When I pressed Haringey Council for an explanation on the racially exclusive nature of the housing plans, Alan Strickland, Haringey Council's cabinet member for housing and regeneration, told me: 'Where people are struggling to access different types of homes because of their incomes, clearly what has to be done is address their incomes. That must come through skills and jobs and training and employment. Through our economic development and jobs work, we want to make absolutely sure that we're improving life chances so that everybody can access these new homes.' It seemed like an unrealistically ambitious cop-out answer in the context of systematic racial economic disadvantage. If we were yet to solve the problem nationally, how on earth was one council going to achieve it? But they've pressed on with their plans. In mid-2016, a source close to Haringey Council told me that they had no intention to make a

U-turn, despite the solid evidence that the plans could lead to black racial displacement.

This is just one borough in one city. But it's a clear example of how, in Britain, race and class are intertwined. In this case, building housing out of reach for working-class people meant that it was out of reach for black people.

We should be rethinking the image we conjure up when we think of a working-class person. Instead of a white man in a flat cap, it's a black woman pushing a pram. It's worth questioning exactly who wins from the suggestion that the only working-class people worth our compassion are white, or that it's black and ethnic minority people who are hoarding scant resources at the expense of white working-class people who are losing out.

A seemingly innocuous phrase has become naturalised in British politics over the last decade. The phrase 'white working class' is supposed to describe a group of disadvantaged and under-represented people in Britain. When she threw her hat in the ring for the 2015 Labour Party leadership contest, Leicester West's MP Liz Kendall explicitly let it be known that she was interested in supporting white working-class children. Setting out her stall for the leadership bid in a meeting with journalists, she said she wanted Labour to 'be doing the best for kids, particularly in white, working-class communities'.[7] It wasn't just class discrimination that was holding these kids back, she seemed to suggest. It was their whiteness.

And when the BBC announced plans to increase the representation of people of colour in their ranks in an attempt to tackle the over-representation of whiteness on- and off-screen, Conservative politician Philip Davies took great umbrage with the decision. Mr Davies was so outraged that he opted to take on Tony Hall, the BBC's Director-General. Confronting Mr Hall in a House of Commons culture, media and sport select committee session, Davies said, 'If I have a white, working-class constituent who wants that opportunity . . . why should they be deprived because you've set these politically correct targets?'[8] Again, the implication was that race and class are two separate disadvantages that are in direct competition with each other. The phrase *white working class* plays into the rhetoric of the far right. Affixing the word 'white' to the phrase 'working class' suggests that these people face structural disadvantage because they are white, rather than because they are working class. These are newly regurgitated old fears of white victimhood, fears that suggest that the real recipients of racism are white people, and that this reverse racism happens because of the unfair 'special treatment' that black people receive. When Philip

Davies MP intervened against positive action at the BBC, he seemed to interpret the work as an attack on his white and working-class constituents rather than a challenge to the BBC's white and middle-class managers and executives.

And so we find ourselves focusing on imaginary reverse racism, rather than legitimate class prejudice. It is extraordinary to see how Nick Griffin's rhetoric about an embattled white working class has been subsumed into the mainstream less than a decade since his political peak. The class privilege of middle- and upper-class people in Britain is not challenged when we focus on the plight of the white working classes. Instead, it shifts the focus of the problem on to black and brown people. The immigrants. There is a scarcity mentality. 'There are many people who feel that the pace of change in their communities has been too fast, and that the government has not properly resourced those particular areas to respond to that change,' said Baroness Sayeeda Warsi in a 2009 episode of BBC *Question Time*. At the time, she was the Conservatives' shadow minister for community cohesion and social action. 'This is not a race debate,' she continued. 'This is a debate about resources.'

Although Baroness Warsi somewhat optimistically sought to change the terms of the debate, the resentment has never stopped being targeted at immigrants. This feeling of scarcity has been fuelled by government policy. Policies like right to buy, which gave council-house tenants the option to buy the property they were living in with a big discount in the 1980s, reduced the amount of Britain's social-housing stock. Even now, councils are struggling to replace property sold. Information tracking sales between 2015 and 2016 showed that for the 12,246 council homes sold to tenants in England under right to buy, just 2,055 replacements began to be built.[9] This is a consequence of government direction, not grasping immigrants hoarding housing.

The answer to ending British people living in poverty and precarious housing will not be found in ending immigration. There isn't any evidence to suggest that if 'my kind' all 'go back to where we came from' life would get any better or easier for poor white people. The same systems and practices that lead to class hierarchy would still stand.

We must ask why politicians only ever approach class and poverty issues when it is in relation to whiteness. When race isn't mentioned, working-class people aren't considered deserving of targeted policies at all. In fact, before all of this white working-class talk, class was a political taboo. When Margaret Thatcher said in 1987 that there was no such thing as society, she solidified a national feeling that it was individual ambition alone that would allow a person to get on in life. Although we as a country are all obsessed with class, we had deluded ourselves for a long time that it didn't matter at all.

But now, I worry that we've too eagerly accepted the far right's agenda of decent hard-working white British people being besieged by immigrants. A 2014 report from market research company Ipsos MORI found that British people thought the foreign-born population of the country was 31 per cent, as opposed to the actual number of 13 per cent.[10] The same report found that the higher your income, the more likely you are to think that immigrants are a drain on public services. Things have switched from berating working-class people for daring to exist, to extending a hand of help to them as long as it's in opposition to those grasping ethnic minorities. Sticking 'white' in front of the phrase working class is used to make assumptions about race, work and poverty that compounds the currency-like power of whiteness.

When it comes to talking about race, diversity, or even the faintest liberally minded hint of inclusion, self-interested white middle-class people seem to find a renewed interest in the advancement of their white working-class counterparts. In the hands of the have-it-alls, the class and race of the have-nots are pitted against each other. This myth of grabby immigrants angling themselves to snatch opportunities from white working-class people couldn't be further from the truth. A report from *The Economist*, combing through data from the Office of National Statistics, found that some of the richest in Britain benefit from services like public transport and the NHS at a significant advantage than their poorer counterparts,[11] proving that those with wealth already do a very good job of hogging resources. The myth of grabby immigrants does, however, work to serve a particular agenda. These are the interests of those who are invested in preserving the current order of things.

This is a classic (and very successful) case of divide and rule. It feels like a cliché to say, but if anyone feeling resentful about their immigrant neighbours took the time to talk to them and find out a bit about their lives, they would almost certainly find that these people do not have everything handed to them on a plate, but instead are living in poor, cramped conditions, likely having left even worse conditions from wherever they've moved from.

Years before this country had a significant black and immigrant presence, there was an entrenched class hierarchy. The people who maintain these class divisions didn't care about those on the bottom rung then, and they don't care now. But immigration blamers encourage you to point to your neighbour and convince yourself that they are the problem, rather than question where wealth is concentrated in this country, and exactly *why* resources are so scarce. And the people who push this rhetoric couldn't care less either way, just as long as you're not pointing the finger at them. It isn't right to suggest that every win for race equality results in a loss for white working-class people. When socially mobile black people manage to penetrate white-dominated spheres, they often try to put provisions in place (like diversity schemes) to bring others up with them. And they're just more *visible* than white people. I see class-based outcry about efforts to boost black representation from people who are in the position to bring up their working-class counterparts if they wanted to. For some reason, they choose not to, yet are quick to block other kinds of progress.

So although class and race are inextricably connected, for people of colour, moving or changing class can be a tantalising prospect. Children of immigrants are often assured by well-meaning parents that educational access to the middle classes can absolve them from racism. We are told to work hard, go to a good university, and get a good job.

We can't berate our parents for wanting us to have a better life and better chances than they did. But after I graduated, I quickly realised that social mobility was not going to save me. My suspicions were backed up by the statistics. When the Trades Union Congress looked at data from the Office for National Statistics Labour Force Survey, they found that black employees were dealing with a growing pay gap in comparison to their white counterparts, and that this pay gap actually *widened* with higher qualifications. Black people with education up to GSCE level were paid 11 per cent less. Black people with A-levels saw an average of 14 per cent less pay, and university-educated black graduates saw a gap of, on average, 23 per cent less pay than their white peers.[12] A cap, gown and degree scroll does nothing to shield black graduates from discrimination.

The children of immigrants have quietly assimilated to demands of colour-blindness, doing away with any evidence of our culture and heritage in an effort to fit in. We've listened to our socially conservative parents, and educated ourselves up to our eyeballs. We've kept our gripes to ourselves, and changed our appearance, names, accents and dress in order to fit the status quo. We have bitten our tongues, exercised safe judgement, and tiptoed around white feelings in an effort to not rock the boat. We've been tolerant up to the point of not even mentioning race, lest we're accused of playing the race card. Forget politician-speak about Britain being a tolerant country. Being constantly looked at like an alien in the country you were born in requires true tolerance.

I don't think that any amount of class privilege, money or education can shield you from racism. And although I don't begrudge kids from poor backgrounds getting the education or training they desire and following their dreams (in fact, I actively encourage it), I want them to know that this alone is not going to end racism, because the onus isn't on them to change people's minds with sharp suits, slick hair and FTSE100 companies.

Moving class requires a modicum of success, and if you're not white, success is a double-edged sword. Even if you work really hard and find yourself at the top of your game, there will be a debate about whether this has happened because of your race, or despite it. When a woman who wasn't white – poet Sarah Howe – won the £20,000 TS Eliot Prize for poetry, satirical magazine *Private Eye* questioned her success, writing: 'as a successful and very "presentable" young woman with a dual Anglo–Chinese heritage, Howe can be seen as a more acceptable ambassador for poetry than the distinguished grumpy old men she saw off.'[13] The suggestion couldn't be clearer: it was an implication that her success was no more than a box-ticking exercise. There is a suspicion laid at the feet of people who aren't white who succeed outside of their designated fields (for black people, those fields are singing and sport). And if you are a young woman, some will think that you have only become successful because an imagined male superior is interested in having sex with you. The reason why you have made it is never assumed to be a result of your hard work, will or determination. There's nothing more threatening to some than the redistribution of cultural capital.

Complicating the idea that race and class are distinctly separate rather than intertwined will be hard work. It involves piercing a million thought bubbles currently dominating conversations about class in this country. It means irritating politicians and commentators, and it means calling their story of a white working class besieged by selfish and ungrateful immigrants exactly what they are – hate-mongering nonsense. Divide and rule serves no useful purpose in the politics of class solidarity, neither does it work particularly well in lifting people out of poverty. We know that targeted policies aimed at eradicating class inequalities will also go some way in challenging race inequalities, because so many black households are low income. But we can't be naive enough to believe that those in power are in any way interested in piercing their power for the sake of a fairer society. And although working-class white and BME people have lots in common, we need to remember that although the experiences are very similar, they are also very different.

Although some deal with class prejudice, others deal with racialised class prejudice. It's that complexity that needs to be navigated successfully if we ever want an accurate understanding of what it means to be working class in Britain today.

7

There's No Justice, There's Just Us

'When do you think we'll get to an end point?'

I'm at a sixth-form college in south London, talking to a large group of teenagers about racism in Britain. The question is put to me by a seventeen-year-old girl. She's echoed on this point by her teacher. They're both white.

'There is no end point in sight,' I reply. 'You can't skip to the resolution without having the difficult, messy conversation first. We're still in the hard bit.'

After my talk, a group of black teenagers crowd around me outside, talking excitedly. 'I think the people who want to skip to an end point are the ones not really affected by the issues,' says one girl. I'm impressed by her insight.

When Barack Obama was elected President of the United States, everyone was quick to crow that we were now living in a post-racial society. But proclaiming post-racial success was a way to bury any discussion of racism – to insist that we had actually pressed fast forward, and everything was OK now.

That there was no need to complain. 'End point' is the new 'post racial'. The narrative has changed ever so slightly. 'Post racial' only acknowledged racism of the past, and insisted that the present was an anti-racist utopia. 'End point' accepts the racism of the present, but doesn't want to dwell on it too much, instead hoping that the post-racist utopia is just around the corner. Both are very reluctant to talk about racism.

I didn't want to disappoint that class of sixth-formers, but there was no happy ending to my speech. Britain's relationship with race and racism isn't a neat narrative with a feel-good resolution. Change is incremental, and racism will exist long after I die. But if you're committed to anti-racism, you're in it for the long haul. It will be difficult. Getting to the end point will require you to be uncomfortable.

In my original blog post of 2014, I spoke about a communication gap that was so frustrating that it pushed me away from talking to white people about race. I still think there is a communication gap, and I'm not sure if we will ever overcome it. Even now, when I talk about racism, the response from white people is to shift the focus away from their complicity and on to a conversation about what it means to be black, and about 'black identity'. They might hand-wring about what they call 'identity politics' – a term now used by the powerful to describe the resistance of the structurally disadvantaged. But they won't properly engage in the conversation, instead complaining that people mustn't divide themselves off into small groups, and that we're all one race, 'the human race'. Discussing racism is not the same thing as discussing 'black identity'. Discussing racism is about discussing white identity. It's about white anxiety. It's about asking why whiteness has this reflexive need to define itself against immigrant bogey monsters in order to feel comfortable, safe and secure. Why am I saying one thing, and white people are hearing something completely different?

Often white people ask me, very earnestly, what I think they should do to help end racism. Anti-racist work – the logistics, the strategy, the organising – needs to be led by the people at the sharp end of injustice. But I also believe that white people who recognise racism have an incredibly important part to play. That part can't be played while wallowing in guilt. White support looks like financial or administrative assistance to the groups doing vital work. Or intervening when you are needed in bystander situations. Support looks like white advocacy for anti-racist causes in all-white spaces. White people, you need to talk to other white people about race. Yes, you may be written off as a radical, but you have much less to lose.

Talk to other white people who trust you. Talk to white people in the areas of your life where you have influence. If you feel burdened by your unearned privilege, try to use it for something, and use it where it counts. But don't be anti-racist for the sake of an audience. Being white and anti-racist in your private or professional life, where there's very little praise to be found, is much more difficult, but ultimately more meaningful. When Jeremy Corbyn MP was elected leader of the Labour Party in 2015, it upset many in the political establishment who felt his politics were far too extreme. As he announced his first shadow cabinet, political commentators suddenly found themselves concerned with the fact that the top jobs – shadow foreign secretary, shadow chancellor and shadow home secretary – had gone to white men. A *Telegraph* column on the topic began: 'The Labour leader is a white man. His deputy leader is a white man. His shadow chancellor is a white man. His shadow foreign secretary is a white man. His shadow home secretary is a white man. Welcome to the new politics.'[1]

This sudden interest in the unbearable whiteness of politics seemed utterly disingenuous to me. This was an example of how the language of liberation causes can be used for political football. When these political commentators discovered anti-racism solely to oppose Jeremy Corbyn, there was no real interest in disrupting the overwhelmingly white political landscape. There was no interest shown in unpacking the race and class standards that marginalise people of colour in the political professions. It was anti-racism for the show of it.

And online, the performative nature of social media anti-racism couldn't have been more apparent than in the wake of the Paris terror attacks. In mid-November 2015, suicide bombers detonated their explosive vests in densely populated areas of Paris, while gunmen walked into two restaurants, a bar and the Bataclan Concert Hall, injuring hundreds and leaving 130 people dead.

The Paris attacks saw an outpouring of grief on social media. Facebook designed a specific statement for its users in Paris to mark themselves as safe from danger. The outpouring of grief led some to ask not just Facebook, but also their peers, why they grieved for some, yet not for others. The answers invariably led to factors like race, development and location – to who does and who doesn't make a 'relatable' victim of terror. And then something very peculiar happened. As the rolling coverage of the Paris attacks continued on traditional news media, the seven-month-old story of terrorist attacks on Kenya's Garissa University was being shared all over Facebook and Twitter. Two days after the Paris attacks, the Garissa University attack had become the most read on the BBC news website. The news organisation's trending team reported, 'About three-quarters of the hits on the story came from social media, rather than from the front page of the BBC news website.' The report on the phenomenon continued, 'Around half of the hits on the story came from North America, with another quarter from the UK. In total, the story attracted more than 10 million page views over two days – or about four times as many as it did when the attack actually happened in April.'[2]

Here, it seemed, was a warped attempt at solidarity with Kenyan people, clumsily wielded to make a point about empathy, race and sympathy after the Paris attacks. It was telling the BBC trending team noted that when the attack happened in April of that year, the reception of social media was utterly lacklustre. The resurfacing of this story in order to elicit grief – or to guilt others who were already grieving – in order to make a point, was nothing but shallow, performative anti-racism. To put it bluntly, Kenyans needed that solidarity, and those social-media shares, back in April. They didn't need it seven months later, in November, as an act of self-important 'proof' that people in the UK and US cared deeply about black and brown countries affected by terrorism in light of press coverage of the Paris attacks. The events in

Kenya were cynically used so that people in the UK and US could prove to themselves and to their friends that they were socially aware. That they were one of the good ones. That they believed that black lives matter.

Solidarity is nothing but self-satisfying if it is solely performative. A safety pin stuck to your lapel after a referendum about the EU that turned into a referendum on immigration is symbolic, but it won't stop someone from getting deported. We really need to be honest with ourselves, and recognise our own inherent biases, before we think about performing anti-racism for an audience.

The perverse thing about our current racial structure is that it has always fallen on the shoulders of those at the bottom to change it. Yet racism is a white problem. It reveals the anxieties, hypocrisies and double standards of whiteness. It is a problem in the psyche of whiteness that white people must take responsibility to solve. You can only do so much from the outside.

After I declared that I no longer wanted to talk to white people about race in 2014, I noticed a sudden upswing in people, white and otherwise, who wanted to hear me talk about race. Everyone wanted to know what I had to say once I had said what I'd always been discouraged from saying. Setting my boundaries had given me a renewed permission to speak.

One thing is consistently clear to me: writing about race taps into a desperate thirst for discussion from those who are affected by the issues. In a way, I can understand that desperation, that feeling of thirst. It's why I started writing. I got into political commentary because I wanted to change that consensus, to widen the narrow confines of political ideas that were deemed acceptable. But over the years I have realised both the necessity and futility of this job. Attempting to challenge the racism deemed acceptable in political discussion is tacitly tolerated, but making white people feel uncomfortable is impermissible.

If you keep up with news and current affairs, you'll find that every day there's a new reason to justify no longer talking to white people about race. There is so much injustice, and there are so many reasons to keep your despair about it to yourself. You might see it, but you won't dare speak it, for fear of social sanctions. Since I wrote a blog post declaring that I no longer wanted to talk to white people about race, I have come to realise that I'm not alone in my despair. I have come to realise that there are thousands fighting this battle every day. People who want to dismantle racism don't need to be persuaded or cajoled.

I know that, at first, talking about race is uncomfortable, because too many white people are angry and in denial. And I understand that after white people begin to get it, it's even more uncomfortable for them to think about how their whiteness has silently aided them in life. A lifetime learning to empathise with white people's stories means that I get it. But I don't want white guilt. Neither do I want to see white people wasting precious time profusely apologising rather than actively doing things. No useful movements for change have ever sprung out of fervent guilt.

Instead, get angry. Anger is useful. Use it for good. Support those in the struggle, rather than spending too much time pitying yourself. Unlike white people, people of colour don't often ask me for advice on what I think they should do to fight racism. Instead, they ask me if I have any good strategies for coping. I don't have any magic formulas, but I'm a big advocate for setting boundaries when needed. Surround yourself with people who you can draw strength from. If you need to stop talking to white people about race, don't feel guilty about it. Rest and recharge, so that you're ready to do your anti-racist work in a sustainable way. I don't want anyone of any race, when faced with the insurmountable task of challenging racism, to collapse into despondency. As a long-time depressive I know how much it can paralyse, how the feeling of hopelessness works to utterly crush creativity, and passion, and drive. But those are the three things that we will definitely need if we're ever going to end this injustice. We have to fight despondency. We have to hang on to hope.

In a world where blunt, obvious acts are just the tip of the iceberg of racism, we need to describe the invisible monolith. Now, racism can be found in the way a debate is framed. Now, racism can be found in coded language. Attacking racist frame, form, functions and codes with no words to describe them can make you feel like you are the only one who sees the problem. We need to see racism as structural in order to see its insidiousness. We need to see how it seeps, like a noxious gas, into everything.

In a conversation about structural racism, a friend of mine once made a point that was both glaringly obvious and painfully elusive. Structures, she said, are made out of people. When we talk about structural racism, we are talking about the intensification of personal prejudices, of groupthink. It is rife. But rather than deeming the current situation an absolute tragedy, we should seize it as an opportunity to move towards a collective responsibility for a better society, taking account of the internal hierarchies and intersections along the way.

It doesn't have to be like this, and the solution starts with us. Racism's cultural reach is so pervasive that we must take up the mantle of changing our workplaces and social circles ourselves. Often in these conversations, someone will pipe up to say in order to win, we need unity. But I think that if we wait for unity, we'll be waiting for ever. People are always going to disagree about the finer points of progress. Waiting for unity is just inviting inertia.

So, a word to those who feel the weight of racism, who keenly feel the effects of how it suffocates kindness, and generosity, and potential. How it is slowing down the world we live in. We cannot escape the legacies of the past, but we can use them to model our future. The late Terry Pratchett once wrote 'there's no justice. Just us.' I can't think of any other phrase that best sums up the task ahead.

It's on your shoulders and mine to dismantle what we once accepted to be true. It's our task. It needs to be done with whatever resources we have on hand. We need to change narratives. We need to change the frames. We need to claim the entirety of British history. We need to let it be known that black is British, that brown is British, and that we are not going away. We can't wait for a hero to swoop in and make things better. Rather than be forced to react to biased agendas, we should outright reject them and set our own. Most importantly, we must survive in this mess, and we do that any way we can.

If you are disgusted by what you see, and if you feel the fire coursing through your veins, then it's up to you. You don't have to be the leader of a global movement or a household name. It can be as small scale as chipping away at the warped power relations in your workplace. It can be passing on knowledge and skills to those who wouldn't access them otherwise. It can be creative. It can be informal. It can be your job. It doesn't matter what it is, as long as you're doing something.

AFTERMATH

This book is nothing without the political climate that greeted it.

The events of 2016 caused a state of shell shock for progressives across the western world. It began with Britain voting to leave the European Union – a symbol of continental unity – in June 2016, and ended with the election of an unqualified, unpredictable opportunist, Donald Trump, in November of that year. Among progressive circles, it felt like we spent the beginning of 2017 agonising over Trump and Brexit. If we weren't agonising, we were using these electoral gains as a reason to organise, a point to stand against. Because these seemingly unexpected political gains happened in both Britain and America, they dominated conversation. But they were part of a political trend that was totally encompassing Europe – a lurch to the far right. We should have seen it coming.

Almost a decade on from the global financial crisis, during which the vast majority of people had been living with prolonged financial insecurity, an old kind of politics emerged. Brutal, punitive strong man values were back on the agenda. The resurgence of the fascist, violently anti-immigrant group Golden Dawn in Greece, a country hit hard by the financial crash, was testament to this; by 2015, Golden Dawn had become the country's third largest political party, with far reaching tentacles in the judiciary and police force. Late 2015 saw Switzerland's anti-immigrant Swiss People's Party win the biggest share of vote in the federal election. In the Netherlands, Geert Wilders' far right Party for Freedom topped political opinion polls in 2016. The same year saw Sweden's white nationalist Sweden Democrats, with roots in neo-Nazism, become the country's third biggest political party. In France's 2016 presidential election, Marine Le Pen and her far right party Front National were so successful that they made it into the final round of a two candidate race, losing with a 34 per cent share of the vote. The unstoppable tide of European far right electoral gains also took place in Cyprus, Denmark, Austria, Slovakia, Germany, Italy, Greece and Hungary. Their archaic, regressive values were demonstrated in the success of Finland's Finns Party, who won second place in the 2015 election. According to the BBC, their 2011 manifesto suggested that young white Finnish women turn away from education to concentrate on providing the next generation of Finnish workers – thereby circumventing any need for immigrant labour.[1] In the white nationalist revolution, a woman's place is barefoot and pregnant in the kitchen.

These politicians grasped at public opinion amid the backdrop of the catastrophic migrant crisis, reaching its worst in 2015. A vicious civil war in Syria saw almost five and a half million of the country's population registering abroad as refugees, according to the UN Refugee Agency. But across Europe, governments were largely ambivalent to their needs. Some helped. Germany took in a million refugees in 2015. Other countries were less giving. Rather than extending an arm of compassion, in 2016, Hungary's government published a booklet suggesting that allowing migrants to settle would endanger the country's culture and traditions.[2] Angela Merkel was harshly criticised for her compassion by far right political party Alternative for Germany, and their berating of her helped them climb in the polls.

It felt like everywhere, public opinion was veering towards hostility. The drawbridges came up and the atmosphere turned sharp. Every country was full, and every country had to look after their own. The world had turned inward. Politics had become punitive, rather than empathetic and generous. Refugees were dying in capsized dinghy boats in the Mediterranean Sea, and populist politics told us not only to look away, but somehow that people fleeing war and poverty did not need our help. We were too stretched. And how desperate could they really be if some of them had mobile phones?

Racism has always been on my mind, but I recognise that that's not always been the case for other people of colour in Britain. That changed after the Brexit vote. British citizens were told to 'go home', while visitors on visas were told by sneering ill-wishers that their time here was up. Nigel Farage of UKIP seemed to be on the television constantly, pretending to be representative of the average Brit while clutching a pint in a pub, or standing in front of a campaign bus declaring Britain had reached breaking point because of migration. In the United States, the burgeoning Black Lives Matter movement had gone global, with the new technology of smartphones shining a harsh light on long running injustices inflicted by law enforcement onto black communities, the blurry footage posted on social media, igniting the righteous rage of a new generation of activists. America was barely impacted by the refugee crisis, but it didn't stop Donald Trump describing Mexicans as the creeping 'black threat' I'd discussed in chapter 4, using his presidential campaign to call for building a wall to keep them out (the infamous quote: 'They're bringing drugs. They're bringing crime. They're rapists. And some, I assume, are good people'[3]). Meanwhile, fringe hate website Breitbart settled into the heart of global power when Trump appointed executive chairman Steve Bannon as his chief strategist shortly after Trump was elected president. Nigel Farage boasted about meeting with Trump[4], and Marine Le Pen was spotted in Trump Tower[5]. Not only was the malignant political force of the far right – considered defeated after World War Two – making a triumphant comeback, but it appeared to be forming allegiances.

The whole thing was a horror show. The same ideologies I had taken to task in the book were happening in real life. White genocide theory, inherent to the ideology of the far right, was back. Every far right electoral gain was paired with ethno-nationalism and accusations that migrants and refugees were threats to national unity. In chapter 4, I'd written about fear of a black planet and the inherent misogyny of white nationalism – then Finland's far right swept into power with their eyes on white women's wombs. I'd written about multiculturalism becoming a dirty word, of scaremongering and white victimhood – and suddenly these political strategies were all a part of our politics, enveloping our everyday chat. Brexit and Trump were two electoral blows to progressive politics that loosely sandwiched two years of despair.

In chapter 6, I had analysed how a council in north east London had de-prioritised the needs of social housing tenants as an example of how race and class were intricately linked. Just two weeks after the publication of this book, I, and the rest of the country, watched in hopelessness and mourning as seventy-one residents of Grenfell Tower were incinerated in their own homes. Survivors of the fire lost family members and everything they owned. It was a sickening case study of some of the most marginalised people in Britain: working class people, immigrant families, white pensioners with disabilities, foreigners, school children, recent migrants, people who had made England their home for decades. The death toll took so long to determine that the country identified the victims from the makeshift missing person posters plastered across west London. Transfixed by 24-hour rolling news, I wondered how local government could have failed these people so catastrophically. It was eerie to have made an analysis of race, class and social housing so close to the Grenfell Tower tragedy, to watch the de-prioritising of human lives that I identified in the book play out on television in a burning high rise building. I feel guilty even now drawing links to it, an overtly political tragedy that I want to be wary of politicising lest I trample insensitively over heartbreak.

All of the above: this was the climate that the book entered the world into. My thinking on race had remained consistent for half a decade, and was considered wildly radical back in 2012. But by 2017, the politics of the western world had changed drastically. People were looking for answers – a balm to soothe, or an antidote to fight back.

My initial aim with this book was simple. I wanted to change the national conversation about race. By the time the book was published, the stars had aligned in such a way that people were ready for it. At the turn of 2017, I was full of apprehension about how it would be received. I had decided, with encouragement from my editor, to stick to the same title as the original blog post. It was important to me to be totally honest with readers about that initial flash point of frustration and despair. I knew things were about to get real when I saw the draft book cover. Greg Heinemann, Bloomsbury's design wizard, had, on reading the blog post, translated the words into an image that couldn't be more suited. When I posted the cover to social media, roughly a year before publication, the shares were out of control, and the anticipation was palpable. Much of this response was thanks to that cardinal sin – judging a book by its cover. At the very least it says 'this has not been written by a white person'. At the very most, it says to white audiences 'this is not for you'. And, like a red rag to a bull, the attention came in droves. It enthralled some, and sent others into a rage. In amongst the praise were early signs of ire from white people; some lectured me about segregation, or told me that Martin Luther King Junior would never approve of my work. Others admonished me for my prejudice.

Passionate responses to the way this book looks have never really slowed down. I've heard stories from booksellers who have had the book on display in their window, and stories from readers who have read my book on their daily commute. In every instance, a white person tried to start an argument with them about what they were reading or selling. This was the scenario an east London bookseller relayed to me after I visited her shop to sign some books. An elderly white man had entered the shop, saw the book in the window, and, shaking with rage, proceeded to make a scene at the counter, angry because 'it wouldn't be allowed the other way round'. 'He was so angry, I couldn't speak to him', she told me. Then there was the young black man who, on reading the book in public, had to endure the displeasure of a white woman approaching him to let him know that the book he was reading 'really didn't help the conversation'. White middle class people can be particularly calculated with their discomfort. I have had a lot of people working on the periphery of the book – booksellers, photographers, producers – earnestly tell me that my work is provocative. 'It's very controversial, isn't it?' they'll ask, over and over again, in the space of a thirty minute conversation. 'Is it?' I'll respond. 'Have you read it?' 'No', they will inevitably say.

Beyond the public's gut reaction to the cover, I was keen to see if the content of the book would have an impact on Britain's discussion on race. It's never not scary to present your ideas to the public, ready to be picked apart. But the initial reactions were positive. A day before the book published, a four-thousand-word extract was printed in the *Guardian*. My inbox filled with reader reactions, from heartfelt and reflective to the utterly confusing. One person recommended that I take up yogic flying, assuring me that once I learnt how to levitate, racism might not bother me anymore. But beyond the absurd was a trend. I watched white people reflect on the dynamics of their own lives, and start to consider how race had shaped it. I watched as the book dislodged a pressure valve for readers of colour, who told me that it had given them the confidence to give up on a belligerent friend, or have a difficult conversation with a boss.

The first event for the book took place at London's Southbank centre, three months before publication – a conversation between myself and journalist Hannah Pool. My throat constricted in anxiety as I watched the queue to enter the venue snake down the stairs half an hour before it was due to begin. My friends in the audience told me afterwards that the atmosphere was 'electric'. After forty-five minutes of me discussing my frustrations with white people centring their feelings, we opened up to questions. A white woman raised her hand, began to talk, and promptly burst into tears. I had seen it coming, had heard her voice begin to wobble. She felt terrible about all of this, she said. She had considered self-harm. She didn't know what to do. Gritting my teeth, I cut her off mid-monologue and confidently asserted that wallowing in despair would not get us anywhere. As I felt the pressure mount on me to steer the atmosphere of the room, I realised I was about to become responsible for a lot of people's feelings.

So much of touring this book has involved the regulating of other people's feelings. At book events there have been happy tears, guilty tears, laughter and rage. There has been a tendency for audience frustration to be aimed at whatever heritage venue has been hosting me – legitimate anger at the fact that this is one of the few times these institutions have properly engaged with the topic. There have been inspiring children and teenagers in the audience, genuinely giving me hope for the future. There has been in-real-life trolling in the form of a man who turned up to an event alone, ignored everything I said, and proceeded to follow me around after the book signing was finished, not allowing me to sit quietly or eat in peace, hurling question after question until my publicist told him to go away.

This book arrived at a time when a lot of people were despairing about the political direction of the world. When I take the time to read back over it,

I can't help but dwell on the chapter on feminism. In it, I recalled an early 2014 blog post in which I lamented the lack of any discussion of race that wasn't steeped in colour-blindness. 'Think about the last time you heard a comprehensive discussion about the nature of structural racism in the mainstream media', I had written. '. . . These issues just don't get the kind of airtime that feminism does in the UK press.' My assessment back then wasn't wrong. Coverage in the mainstream was few and far between. Britain is a country that has a very poor record of investing in anti-racist journalists, and it is a country where black academics are numbered in the dozens rather than the thousands. I can count on one hand books of a similar tradition that have been published in Britain in the last three decades by publishing houses with the budget to increase their chances of success. We relied heavily on the American narrative as a tool to find ourselves.

I can't believe how much has changed since then. There has been a renaissance of black critical thought and culture. Whether it has come from companies with big budgets or creative individuals using social media, it feels like the critical anti-racist perspective is on top of a wave, kept afloat by a groundswell of support. Fashion magazine British *Vogue* – an institution in itself – appointed its first ever black male editor. An interview given by Alexandra Shulman, then the magazine's outgoing editor, involved a question asking why, under her leadership, the magazine had a diversity problem. She responded with an insistence that she was 'against quotas' and that her *Vogue* simply included the people she thought were 'interesting'[6] – who just happened to be overwhelmingly white. She hasn't got a racist bone in her body, she said, plus her grandson had a relative who was a civil rights leader, so the suggestion was deeply offensive to her. On reception by the public and her fashion peers, her comments were widely panned, with fashion website *Racked* calling the interview 'a case study in white privilege'.[7] I'm convinced that this critical response wouldn't have happened even as recently as five years ago. There was the success of *Get Out*, an American horror film detailing the subtleties of white, liberal, fetishising racism, and there was Lubaina Himid, the first black woman to win the Turner Prize with artwork addressing slavery and the legacy of colonialism. The Tate Modern put on an unstoppably successful exhibition on art in the age of black power. When both Prime Minister Theresa May and Leader of the Opposition Jeremy Corbyn spent a little bit of their 2017 expressing a commitment to ending race inequality, I understood that anti-racism was no longer on the margins – that public opinion was turning it into a political priority. My little book was longlisted and shortlisted for prestigious awards, and earned a spot on 'best books of 2017' lists. Jo Swinson MP, the deputy leader of the Liberal Democrats, posted about it on social media, calling it a 'brilliant read'.[8] This dynamic of the conversation feels new to me. I'm proud to have contributed to a renewed sense of urgency. If anything, I hope that the success of this book means I become part of a contemporary British crowd, rather than a stand-alone voice.

None of this means that overt or structural racism is over. Donald Trump is still president of the United States, and far right white-nationalist groups around the world are encouraged by his success.[9] They think that everyone will give in to the politics of hate; that they will succeed in taking the world away from the rest of us. Electorally, there has been little climb-down from the far right gains of 2016. But I do believe that there is a difference between ignorance and malice – even though the former can very much feel like (and descend into) the latter. When it comes to the middle ground, I think the side of anti-racist progress is winning. I'm filled with hope, and a kind of political nourishment, when I hear the conversations that come to the fore during my events. Every time I do one I see the audience as a hub of knowledge and potential. I see change. I see talent. It's there in the crowd, buzzing in the atmosphere. I learn a lot, too, from the people of colour who turn up, who are experts in their respective fields and have taken on the additional job of 'anti-racist in the room' at work. Sometimes at these Q&A's I think there are people in the audience who are far more qualified than me to answer specific questions. This is the power of the collective. We've reached a tipping point, and I'm glad that my book has served as catalyst. My dream is that the people who turn up to my events take that opportunity to meet each other, swap details and form their local resistance.

I consider myself to be part of a movement, and I think that if you are deeply touched by what you read in this book, then you are part of that movement too. It's happening right now.

NOTES

Preface

1   This 1994 documentary about race was championed by Oprah at the time of its release. It's a powerful watch.

1: Histories

1   The *Brooks* slave-ship drawing, contributed by Bristol Museum, *A History of the World in 100 Objects*, BBC & The British Museum, http://www.bbc.co.uk/ahistoryofthe world/objects/Akxq5WxwQOKAF5S1ALmKnw

2   'Ports of the Transatlantic Slave Trade', conference paper given by Anthony Tibbles at the TextPorts conference, Liverpool Hope University College, April 2000.

3   *Britain's Forgotten Slave Owners*, episodes 1 & 2, David Olusoga and University College London, first broadcast on BBC2 July 2015.

4   Popularised in the 1980s, the concept of political blackness was used by anti-racism activists to describe anyone who wasn't white, in the spirit of solidarity.

5   'Remember the World as Well as the War: Why the Global Reach and Enduring Legacy of the First World War Still Matter Today', British Council, 2013, page 12.

6   Egypt, France, Germany, India, Russia, Turkey, United Kingdom.

7   'Why the Indian soldiers of WW1 were forgotten', Shashi Tharoor, BBC News Magazine, 2 July 2015, http://www. bbc.co.uk/news/magazine-33317368

8   'A White Man's War? World War One and the West Indies,' Glenford D. Howe, BBC History, 3 October 2011,

http://www.bbc.co.uk/history/worldwars/wwone/west_indies_01.shtml

9 'Riots on the streets of Cardiff as poverty hits', Wales Online, 7 July 2009.

10 'The Roots of Racism in City of Many Cultures', *Liverpool Echo*, 3 August 2005.

11 National Archives, Spotlights on History, 'Demobilisation in Britain, 1918–20', www.nationalarchives.gov.uk/pathways/firstworldwar/spotlights/demobilisation.htm

12 *Mother Country: Britain's Black Community on the Home Front, 1939–45*, Stephen Bourne, The History Press, 2010, page 17.

13 *Staying Power: The History of Black People in Britain*, Peter Fryer, Pluto Press, 1984, page 326.

14 *The Keys*, courtesy of the British Library, The League of Coloured Peoples, 1933, http://www.bl.uk/learning/citizenship/campaign/myh/newspapers/gallery1/paper2/thekeys2.html

15 *The Keys*, courtesy of the British Library, The League of Coloured Peoples, 1933, http://www.bl.uk/learning/citizenship/campaign/myh/newspapers/gallery1/paper5/thekeys5.html

16 By the advent of the Second World War, Dr Moody had married a white woman, Olive Tranter. They had six children, and his son, Charles Arundel 'Joe' Moody, was not only old enough to fight, but keen to do so. But when he went to sign up, he was told by a white army officer that it wasn't possible, because he wasn't of 'pure European descent'. Outraged, Dr Moody used *The Keys* to campaign, and allied with other black organisations for maximum clout. His lobbying of the Colonial Office – a government department that dealt solely with affairs of Empire – led to the decision being overturned in October 1939. Joe was the second black commissioned officer ever to serve in the British Army.

17 There were very few black women in port cities due to the gendered nature of military and ship work.

18 *Report on an Investigation into the Colour Problem in Liverpool and Other Ports*, Liverpool: Association for the Welfare of Half-Caste Children, Muriel Fletcher, 1930.

19 'The Fletcher Report 1930: A Historical Case Study of Contested Black Mixed Heritage Britishness', Mark Christian, *Journal of Historical Sociology*, Volume 21, Issue 2–3, pages 213–241, June/September 2008.

20 *Empire Windrush* 1948, Exploring 20th Century London, Renaissance London Museum, http://www.20thcentury-london.org.uk/empire-windrush-1948.

21 Peach, Ceri, 'Patterns of Afro-Caribbean Migration and Settlement in Great Britain: 1945–1981'. In Brock, Colin, *The Caribbean in Europe: Aspects of the West Indian Experience in Britain, France and the Netherlands*, London: Frank Cass & Co. pp. 62–84.

22 Immigration Patterns of Non-UK Born Populations in England and Wales in 2011, Office for National Statistics, 17 December 2013.

23 'White Riot: The Week Notting Hill Exploded', Mark Olden, *Independent*, 28 August 2008.

24 *Chambers 21st Century Dictionary*, ed. Mairi Robinson, Cambridge University Press.

25 'Notting Hill Riots – 50 years on', Alice Bhandhukravi, BBC.co.uk, 21 August 2008.

26 'White Riot: The Week Notting Hill Exploded', Mark Olden, *Independent*, 28 August 2008.

27 'After 44 Years Secret Papers Reveal Truth About Five Nights of Violence in Notting Hill', *Guardian*, 24 August 2002.

28 Race Discrimination Bill 1960, Parliamentary Archives, HL/PO/PU/2/119.

29 'The Race Relations Act 1965 – Blessing or Curse?', Jenny Bourne, Institute of Race Relations, 13 November 2015, www.irr.org.uk/news/the-race-relations-act-1965-blessing-or-curse/

30 UK Government summary of immigration acts, The Immigration Acts, gov.uk https://www.gov.uk/government/uploads/system/uploads/attachment_data/file/268009/immigrationacts.pdf

31 '1965: New UK race law "not tough enough"', BBC: On This Day, bbc.co.uk, 8 December 1965, http://news.bbc.co.uk/onthisday/hi/dates/stories/december/8/newsid_4457000/4457112.stm

32 'The Origins of the Race Relations Act', Philip N. Soben, Centre for Research in Ethnic Relations, University of Warwick, September 1990, research paper, page 1.

33 *Population*, Edition No.: Social Trends 41, ed. Jen Beaumont, Palgrave Macmillan, UK Office for National Statistics, 2011, page 3.

34 '1968: Race discrimination law tightened', BBC: On This Day, bbc.co.uk, 26 November 1968.

35 BBC *Newsnight* report on the Bristol bus boycott, 27 August 2013.

36 'Protest Revealed City Had Its Own "Dream"', *Bristol Post*, 27 August 2013.

37 'Stop and search: what can we learn from history?', *BBC History Magazine*, Wednesday 12 August 2009, http://www.historyextra.com/feature/stop-and-search-what-can-we-learn-history

38 *Policing the Crisis: Mugging, the State, and Law and Order* (Critical Social Studies), 30 April 1978, Stuart Hall (author), Brian Roberts (contributor), John Clarke (contributor), Tony Jefferson (contributor), Chas Critcher (contributor), Macmillan Press, p. 40.

39 'The Power to Stop and Search', bbc.co.uk, 14 December 2000.

40 'Black People Still Far More Likely to be Stopped and Searched by Police than Other Ethnic Groups', *Independent*, 6 August 2015.

41 *Ethnic Unemployment in Britain (1972–2012)*, Yaojun Li, Runnymede Trust/ University of Manchester Institute for Social Change, January 2014, http://www.runnymedetrust.org/blog/ethnic-unemployment-in-britain

42 *Network – Paint it Black: A Portrait of Handsworth*, Part 2, 1982, LBC / IRN Digitisation Archive, Global Radio UK Ltd. Radio documentary, first broadcast on BRMB Radio Birmingham in 1982.

43 'The Legacy of the Brixton Riots', bbc.co.uk, 5 April 2006.

44 '1981: Brixton Riots Report Blames Racial Tension', bbc.co.uk, 26 November 1981.

45 *Violent Racism: Victimization, Policing and Social Context*, Benjamin Bowling, Oxford University Press, 1999, page 53.

46 Newham Monitoring Project Annual Report 1983, courtesy of the Black Cultural Archives, page 22.

47 'Neighbourhood policing: Past, Present and Future, A Review of the Literature', Police Foundation, Abie Longstaff, James Willer, John Chapman, Sarah Czarnomski and John Graham, May 2015, page 9.

48 Camden Committee for Community Relations Annual Report 1984, courtesy of the Black Cultural Archives, page unknown.

49 Essays written by cadets at the Metropolitan Police Training School, Hendon, 1982. Courtesy of the Black Cultural Archives.

50 'Police Racism and Union Collusion: the John Fernandes Case', National Convention of Black Teachers, year unknown, page 31.

51 *Labour Party Black Sections: Here to stay! The Vauxhall Experience*, Vauxhall Labour Party, 1984, page 1.

52 Bernie Grant at Labour Party Conference, 1984. Archived by Bishopsgate Library.

53 *Darcus Howe on Black Sections in the Labour Party*, Race Today Publications, Black Rose Press, 1985, page 8.

54 'Police Blamed Over 1985 Cherry Groce Brixton Shooting', bbc.co.uk, 10 July 2014.

55 'This is the room where police shot my mum, Cherry Groce', interview by Simon Israel, Channel 4 News, Thursday 10 July 2014.

56 BBC Archive: '1985: Riots in Brixton after police shooting', bbc.co.uk, 28 September 1985.

57 'Riots in Brixton after police shooting', *Guardian* archive, 30 September 1985.

58 *The Killing of Constable Keith Blakelock: The Broadwater Farm Riot*, Tony Moore, Waterside Press, 2015, page 103.

59 'The Broadwater Farm uprising', Stafford Scott, tottenhamrights.org.uk, 28 February 2014.

60 Report of the independent inquiry into disturbances of October 1985 at the Broadwater Farm Estate, Tottenham, chaired by Lord Gifford QC, Broadwater Farm Inquiry 1986, pages 76, 84.

61 'Cherry Groce Inquest: "Astonishing" Police Failures Blamed for 1985 Brixton Riots Trigger Shooting', *International Business Times*, 10 July 2014.

62 'Inner cities policy and problems: regeneration of Liverpool and London; Docklands Urban Development Corporation', Archbishop of Canterbury's Commission on Urban Priority Areas, part 7, The National Archives, Kew 1985–86.

63 *Selma* star David Oyelowo: 'I had to leave Britain to have an acting career', *Radio Times*, 7–13 February 2015.

2: The System

1 'Condon's Apology is Not Enough, Say Lawrences', *Independent*, 1 October 1998.

2 'Lawrence Family Unimpressed By Police Apology', bbc. co.uk, 17 June 1998.

3 'The Stephen Lawrence Inquiry, Report of an Inquiry', by Sir William Macpherson of Cluny, advised by Tom Cook, The Right Reverend Dr John Sentamu, Dr Richard Stone. Presented to Parliament by the Secretary of State for the Home Department by Command of Her Majesty, February 1999, sections 46.1, 6.34.

4 '30 years of British Social Attitudes self-reported racial prejudice data', NatCen Social Research, 27 May 2014.

5 'Racism on the Rise in Britain', *Guardian*, 27 May 2014.

6 Permanent and Fixed Period Exclusions From Schools and Exclusion Appeals in England, 2011/12, Department for Education, 25 July 2013.

7 The Centre for Market and Public Organisation, Test Scores, Subjective Assessment and Stereotyping of Ethnic Minorities, Simon Burgess and Ellen Greaves, September 2009.

8 Destinations of Key Stage 4 and Key Stage 5 Pupils by Characteristics, 2010/11, Department for Education, 23 July 2013.

9 Equality in HE Statistical Report 2013 Students, Equality Challenge Unit.

10 'The sorry state of "equality" in UK universities', *Times Higher Education*, 11 December 2016, www.timeshigher-education.com/blog/sorry-state-equality-uk-universities

11 'A Test for Racial Discrimination in Recruitment Practice in British Cities', Martin Wood, Jon Hales, Susan Purdon, Tanja Sejersen and Oliver Hayllar, National Centre for Social Research, 2009.

12 Youth Unemployment and Ethnicity, Trades Union Congress report, 2012, pages 6–7.

13 'Have Ethnic Inequalities in Employment Persisted Between 1991 and 2011?', Dynamics of Diversity: Evidence From the 2011 Census, Esrc Centre on

Dynamics of Ethnicity (CoDE), University of Manchester and Joseph Rowntree Foundation, September 2013, page 2.

14 'The numbers in black and white: ethnic disparities in the policing and prosecution of drug offences in England and Wales', Niamh Eastwood, Michael Shiner and Daniel Bear, Release & London School of Economics, 2013, pages 15, 16, 31.

15 'Police and Racism: What Has Been Achieved 10 Years After the Stephen Lawrence Inquiry Report?', Jason Bennetto, Equalities and Human Rights Commission, 2009, pages 5, 29, 39.

16 'Inside Outside – Improving Mental Health Services for Black and Minority Ethnic Communities in England', National Institute for Mental Health in England, 2003, page 40.

17 Independent Inquiry into the death of David Bennett, 2003, page 42.

18 'Black and Minority Ethnic People with Dementia and their Access to Support and Services', Jo Moriarty, Nadira Sharif and Julie Robinson, Social Care Institute for Excellence, March 2011, page 4.

19 'Not-So-Positive Discrimination', *Spiked Online*, 9 August 2006.

20 'Is Football Failing Black Managers?' BBC Sport investigates, Simon Stone, BBC Sport, 16 April 2015.

21 'Oyston: Rooney Rule Would Be Ridiculous', *Blackpool Gazette*, 14 October 2014.

22 'Keith Curle: I've Not Seen Anything to Suggest "Rooney Rule" Would Work', *Guardian*, 3 October 2014.

23 'Rooney Rule "Unnecessary", Says Premier League Chief Scudamore', bbc.co.uk, 14 November 2014.

24 In January 2018, the Football Association announced that it will adopt Rooney rule for all England teams.

25 The Green Park Leadership 10,000, June 2015.

26 'Ethnic Boards Target "Too Ambitious"', *Daily Telegraph*, 3 November 2014.

27 Sir Brian Leveson, President of the Queen's Bench Division, Justice for the 21st Century, Caroline Weatherill Lecture, Isle of Man, 9 October 2015.

28 The story of Dame Linda Dobbs, *First 100 Years*, 8 March 2016, http://first100years.org.uk/the-story-of-dame-linda-dobbs/

29 'City Women Call for Quotas to Combat Sexism', *Financial Times*, 15 January 2015.

30 'Construction Industry Calls for Quotas to Ease Gender Inequality', *Architects' Journal*, 30 January 2013.

31 'Ofsted "Positive Discrimination" Call', BBC News, 7 January 2015.

32 'Police Chief Calls For Positive Discrimination', *Daily Telegraph*, 28 January 2013.

3: What is White Privilege?

1 'Can White Workers Radicals Be Radicalized?', Theodore W. Allen, independent pamphlet, Brooklyn New York, 1967.

2 'How I Started the Diane Abbott Twitter Storm', theguardian.com, 5 January 2012.

3 'Was Diane Abbott's Tweet Racist?', telegraph.co.uk, 5 January 2012.

4 'Abbott, White People and Twitter', labourlist.org, 5 January 2012.

5 'Ethnic Minorities in Politics and Public Life House of Commons Library Briefing Paper', Lukas Audickas, 28 June 2016.

6 'Diane Abbott's Tweet and the Red Herring of Anti-White Racism', theguardian.com, 6 January 2012.

7 'Stephen Lawrence's Family Criticise Police over Alleged Spy Plot', theguardian.com, 2 March 2016.

8 'IS Network: Self-Flagellation and the "Kinky Split"', weeklyworker.co.uk, 13 February 2014.

9   'Safe Space or Free Speech? The Crisis Around Debate at UK Universities', Ian Dunt, theguardian.com, 6 February 2016.

10 'Letter From the Birmingham Jail', 16 April 1963, Martin Luther King, Jr, Martin Luther King, Jr Research and Education Institute.

11 'Into the Melting Pot', *The Economist*, 8 February 2014.

12 'This Rush to Downplay Race Ignores the Truth of Inter-Racial Adoption', theguardian.com, 2 November 2010.

13 'Michael Gove Speech on Adoption In Full', politics. co.uk, 23 February 2012.

4: Fear of a Black Planet

1   'Enoch Powell's "Rivers of Blood" Speech', *Daily Telegraph*, 6 November 2007.

2   I repeatedly contacted Mr Farage to ask him to expand on his thoughts on this topic, but one of his aides told me that he wasn't interested in speaking to me.

3   'Farage "Felt Awkward" on Train', *Evening Standard*, 28 February 2014.

4   'BRIEFING: The EU Immigration System is Immoral and Unfair', voteleavetakecontrol.org, no date listed, http:// www.voteleavetakecontrol.org/briefing_immigration. html

5   'Passport Checks Considered for Pregnant NHS Patients', bbc.co.uk, 11 October 2016.

6   'EU Referendum: Vote Leave Focuses on Immigration', bbc.co.uk, 25 May 2016.

7   'Immigration is Now the Top Issue for Voters in the EU Referendum', Ipsos MORI Political Monitor, ipsos-mori. com, June 2016.

8   'Nick Griffin Posts Address of B&B Case Gay Couple Online', theguardian.com, 19 October 2012.

9   'Rescue Boats? I'd Use Gunships to Stop Migrants', *Sun*, 17 April 2015.

10 Hermione Granger: A Thesis, youtube.com/rosianna, 22 December 2015.

11 *Noughts & Crosses* by Malorie Blackman is a dystopian young-adult fiction book in which a different course of history leads to Africa having a powerful advantage over Europe.

5: THE FEMINISM QUESTION

1   Caroline Criado-Perez, Laura Bates, Allegra McEvedy's perfect hangover food, *Woman's Hour*, BBC Radio 4, first aired 31 December 2013.

2   'Ex-Tory MP Attacks Black Feminist on Twitter', voice-online.co.uk, 6 January 2014.

3   'Ain't I a Woman?', *Anti-Slavery Standard*, 2 May 1863, reproduced at http://www.sojournertruth.org/Library/Speeches/AintIAWoman.htm

4   'Intersectionality is an Icepick', sarahditum.com, 18 October 2012.

5   'In Defence of Caitlin Moran and Populist Feminism', *New Statesman*, 22 October 2012.

6   'There's No Point in Online Feminism if It's an Exclusive, Mean Girls Club', *New Statesman*, 21 March 2013.

7   'The Problem With Privilege-Checking', *New Statesman*, 17 December 2012.

8   'A Lexicon of Social Justice', *Breitbart London*, 24 March 2015.

9   'An A-to-Z Guide to the New PC', *Spectator*, 7 February 2015.

10 'Check My Privilege? I Have, Thanks. You're Still Wrong', *Spectator*, 8 June 2013.

11 'RIP This Britain: With Academic Objectivity, Oxford Professor and Population Expert David Coleman Says

White Britons Could Be in the Minority by the 2060s –
Or Sooner', dailymail.co.uk, 28 May 2016.

12 BBC Radio 4, *Today*, 18 January 2016.

13 Crime Statistics, Focus on Violent Crime and Sexual
Offences, 2012/13 Release, Chapter 2 – Homicide, Office
for National Statistics, 13 February 2014, page 11.

14 An Overview of Sexual Offending in England and
Wales, Ministry of Justice, Home Office & the Office for
National Statistics – Statistics bulletin, 10 January 2013,
page 6.

15 'Jack Straw Criticised for "Easy Meat" Comments on
Abuse', bbc.co.uk, 8 January 2011.

16 'Naomi Campbell: Fashion Industry "Guilty of Racist
Acts"', Channel 4 News, 16 September 2013.

6: RACE AND CLASS

1 'Identity, Awareness and Political Attitudes: Why Are We
Still Working Class?', *British Social Attitudes* 33, Social
Class, NatCen Social Research, 2016, page 2.

2 'A New Model of Social Class: Findings from the BBC's
Great British Class Survey Experiment', *Sociology*,
2 April 2013.

3 'Poverty Among Ethnic Groups: How and Why Does It
Differ?', Guy Palmer and Peter Kenway, Joseph Rowntree
Foundation, 2007, page 5.

4 '2011 Census analysis: Ethnicity and the Labour Market,
England and Wales', Office for National Statistics,
13 November 2014.

5 'London's Demography, Gentrification Blues', *The Economist*, 9 August 2013.

6 *Local Ethnic Inequalities: Ethnic Differences in Education,
Employment, Health and Housing in Districts of England
and Wales, 2001–2011*, University of Manchester in
association with the Runnymede Trust, page 10.

7 'Liz Kendall "Will Back White Working-Class Young"', theguardian.com, 29 May 2015.

8 '"BBC Plan to Promote Ethnic Minorities is Racist", says MP', telegraph.co.uk, 15 July 2014.

9 'Right to Buy Sales: January to March 2016, England', Department for Communities and Local Government, Housing Statistical Release, 30 June 2016.

10 '10 Things We Should Know About Attitudes to Immigration in the UK', Bobby Duffy & Tom Frere-Smith, Ipsos MORI, *Perceptions and Reality*, January 2014.

11 'Sharper Elbows: The Well-Off are Grabbing an Ever-Larger Share of Spending', *The Economist*, 14 November 2015.

12 'Black Workers With Degrees Earn a Quarter Less Than White Counterparts, Finds TUC', tuc.org.uk, 1 February 2016.

13 *Private Eye*, 22 January 2016.

7: There's No Justice, There's Just Us

1 'No Women in Top Jobs? Welcome to the Hypocrisy of the Jeremy Corbyn Era', *Daily Telegraph*, 14 September 2015.

2 'Millions Are Sharing Attack Stories That Aren't About Paris', BBC Trending, 16 November 2015.

Aftermath

1 'Who are the nationalist Finns Party?', Jan Sundberg, bbc.co.uk, 11 May 2015, http://www.bbc.co.uk/news/world-europe-32627013

2 'Expel Hungary from EU for hostility to refugees, says Luxembourg, Matthew Weaver and Patrick Kingsley', theguardian.com, 13 September 2016, https://www.theguardian.com/world/2016/sep/13/expel-hungary-from-eu-for-hostility-to-refugees-says-luxembourg

3 'Here Are All the Times Donald Trump Insulted Mexico', Katie Reilly, time.com, 31 August 2016, http://time.com/4473972/donald-trump-mexico-meeting-insult/

4 'Farage says UK can "do business" with Trump after becoming first British politician to meet President-elect, Lizzie Dearden', independent.co.uk, 12 November 2016, http://www.independent.co.uk/news/world/americas/us-elections/donald-trump-president-us-election-win-nigel-farage-visits-trump-tower-first-british-politician-new-a7413961.html

5 'Marine Le Pen visits Trump Tower in New York, David Lawler and Ruth Sherlock', telegraph.co.uk, 12 January 2017, http://www.telegraph.co.uk/news/2017/01/12/marine-le-pen-visits-trump-tower-new-york/

6 'Former *Vogue* editor Alexandra Shulman: "I find the idea that there was a posh cabal offensive"', Decca Aitkenhead, theguardian.com, 10 November 2017, https://www.theguardian.com/media/2017/nov/10/former-vogue-editor-alexandra-shulman-find-idea-that-there-was-a-posh-cabal-offensive

7 'Alexandra Shulman's *Guardian* Interview Is a Case Study on White Privilege', Nadra Nittle, racked.com, 12 November 2017, https://www.racked.com/2017/11/12/16641058/alexandra-shulman-guardian-interview-british-vogue-racism

8 https://www.instagram.com/p/BbExUv3nwqi/?taken-by=jo_swinson

9 'British Far-Right Group Exults Over Attention From Trump, Dan Bilefsky and Stephen Castle', nytimes.com, 29 November 2017, https://www.nytimes.com/2017/11/29/world/europe/britain-first-trump.html

BIBLIOGRAPHY

Adams, Carol J., *The Sexual Politics of Meat: A Feminist-Vegetarian Critical Theory*, New York: Continuum, 1990

Allen, Theodore W., *The Invention of the White Race, Volume 1: Racial Oppression and Social Control*, London: Verso, 1994

Bourne, Stephen, *Dr Harold Moody*, London: London Borough of Southwark, Southwark Local History Library, 2008

Mother Country: Britain's Black Community on the Home Front 1938–45, Stroud, Gloucestershire: The History Press, 2010

Crenshaw, Kimberlé, *Mapping the Margins: Intersectionality, Identity Politics, and Violence against Women of Color*, Stanford Law Review Vol. 43, No. 6 (July, 1991), pages 1241–99, Stanford, California: Stanford Review, 1991

Das, Santanu, *The Indian Sepoy in the First World War*, London: British Library, https://www.bl.uk/world-war-one/articles/the-indian-sepoy-in-the-first-world-war

de Beauvoir, Simone, *The Second Sex*, New York: Knopf, 1953

Fanon, Frantz, *Black Skin, White Masks*, New York: Grove Press, 1967

Hall, Stuart; Critcher, Chas; Jefferson, Tony; Clarke, John; Roberts, Brian; *Policing the Crisis, Mugging, the State and Law and Order*, London: Macmillan, 1978

hooks, bell, *Ain't I a Woman: Black Women and Feminism*, London: Pluto Press, 1987

Lorde, Audre, *Sister Outsider: Essays and Speeches*, Trumansburg, New York: Crossing Press, 1984

Spelman, Elizabeth V., *Inessential Woman: Problems of Exclusion in Feminist Thought*, Boston: Beacon Press, 1990

Vaughan, David A., *Negro Victory: The Life Story of Dr Harold Moody*, London: Independent Press Ltd, 1950

Wallace, Michele, *Black Macho and the Myth of the Superwoman*, New York: Dial Press, 1979.

ACKNOWLEDGEMENTS

Thank you to Rupert for taking a chance on me, and to Alexa von Hirschberg and Angelique Tran Van Sang for turning me into a better writer. To everyone at Bloomsbury who believed in this book, I hope I've done you proud.

To Jessica and Jenny, who both bared your souls to me for the purposes of this book, I can't thank you enough for being so honest with me.

Thank you to John Fernandes and others who were indispensably helpful with my research.

Thank you to those who pointed me in the right direction for research along the way: Kirsty, Aisling and Yasmin.

CC, your support has made this happen. You're my backbone.

INDEX

A NOTE ON THE AUTHOR

RENI EDDO-LODGE is a London-based, award-winning journalist. She has written for the *New York Times*, the *Voice, Daily Telegraph, Guardian, Independent, Stylist,* the *Pool, Dazed and Confused*, and the *New Humanist. Why I'm No Longer Talking to White People about Race* is her first book.

renieddolodge.co.uk
@renireni

A NOTE ON THE TYPE

The text of this book is set in Linotype Sabon, a typeface named after the type founder, Jacques Sabon. It was designed by Jan Tschichold and jointly developed by Linotype, Monotype and Stempel in response to a need for a typeface to be available in identical form for mechanical hot-metal composition and hand composition using foundry type.

Tschichold based his design for Sabon roman on a font engraved by Garamond, and Sabon italic on a font by Granjon. It was first used in 1966 and has proved an enduring modern classic.

Made in the USA
San Bernardino, CA
12 June 2020

73274824R00178